AMERICA'S #1 CHRISTIAN SUCCESS COACH

DR. DAVE MARTIN

THE

FORCE

OF

FAVOR

SEVEN

WAYS TO

INCREASE

YOUR FAVOR

HARRISON HOUSE PUBLISHING

11 12 13 14 15 / 23 22 21 20

The Force of Favor
ISBN: 978-160683-353-7
Copyright © 2012 by Dave Martin

Published by:
Harrison House Publishers

CONTENTS

FOREWORD

God doesn't have "Favor-ites"...His favor is available for everybody!

The "favor" of God can be somewhat of a mystery, and yet I believe it doesn't have to be. In Proverbs 8 we read that, "For whoever finds me finds life and obtains FAVOUR from the Lord..." God is a God of favor and He lavishes his love and grace on those who walk with Him. The truth is, God blesses those who walk in faithfulness!

Over many years, Bobbie and I have watched the favor of God in our lives, on our family and in our ministry. We are so grateful for the favor of God - the overgenerous kindness of a Father that loves His children and wants what is best for them.

Dr. Dave Martin is a gift to the Body of Christ. His heart to help churches, his understanding of the Word of God and his commitment to biblical teaching in the area of finance and faith has brought freedom to many. As a family, the Martins have learned what it means to live within the will of God, attracting favor that is life-giving and generous.

You see, favor isn't just for us. The Bible says, "I will bless you and make your name great THAT you will be a blessing" (Genesis). When we attract the favor of God, when we find ourselves living in overflow, we must then extend our hand to others. I love being around people who have the favor of God!

As you read this book, may you find the *Force of Favor* in your marriage, in your work and in your walk with God.

There is no substitute for the favor of the Lord.

Brian Houston
Senior Pastor, Hillsong Church

WHAT OTHERS ARE SAYING

"We all want to live in favor, and we all need God's favor in our lives. In *The Force of Favor*, Dr. Dave unpacks how favor can be activated in our lives and how we can live the abundant life God has purposed for us. I highly recommend that you give this book to everyone you know!"

Christine Caine
International Speaker
Founder–The A21 Campaign

"Dr. Dave Martin is an incredibly anointed life coach. The nuggets shared in his book, *The Force of Favor*, have greatly impacted our church. As you read this book, expect God's favor to increase in your life!"

Jentezen Franklin
Acclaimed Author of "Fasting"
Pastor–Free Chapel, Gainesville, GA
Pastor–Free Chapel, Irvine, CA

"The favor of God is the outworking of God's grace. Favor is not something we are entitled to... but it's something we are invited to. Dr. Dave Martin has a unique ability to communicate God's favor in a way that will help you to experience an increasing 'flow of favor' in your life!"

Kevin Gerald
Celebrated Author
Pastor–Champions Centre
Tacoma, Washington

"The Bible tells us Jesus grew in favor with God and in favor with people...*The Force of Favor* will teach YOU how to grow in favor as well. Dr. Dave Martin gives powerful, practical steps on how to multiply favor in your life–just as I have seen displayed in his own life."

Leon Fontaine
CEO–The Miracle Channel
Pastor–Springs Church, Winnipeg, Canada

WHY I WROTE
THIS BOOK

In case you don't know it yet, I'm a churchgoer. I love to go to church. I love to worship. I love to pray. I love to sing and exalt the Lord. I teach in a lot of churches, too. In fact, I travel all over the world, teaching in more than a hundred churches each year. I also teach in secular and academic settings, but the thrust of my speaking always has been and always will be the local church.

When I'm not teaching in a church, I'm listening to teaching. I'm sitting somewhere near the front of my home church or some other church I might be visiting during one of my frequent trips and I'm listening to the minister proclaim and explain the various truths of God's Word. Consequently, I have heard a lot of sermons on a lot of different topics over the years. One of the subjects that seems to be echoing from many of America's pulpits today is the subject of favor. I have particularly heard a lot of teachings on the Old Testament Year of Jubilee, especially as that monumental event on the Jewish calendar relates to God's various promises of deliverance, blessing, and kindness.

I have been stirred by these messages, so I resolved some time ago to develop my own teaching on the Year of Jubilee. The great sermons of other pastors had inspired me, and, over time, I had gleaned my own insights and revelations that I wanted to share on the subject, incorporating with them the ideas that I had received from other anointed men and women of God.

In case you don't know, great sermons are "birthed." They don't just happen during an afternoon of focused study prior to a Sunday service. Most powerful sermons begin in the heart of a minister in much the same way that human life begins in the womb. All human life begins as a single cell, which then grows and multiplies until it becomes a self-sustaining life that is capable of supporting its own weight. Similarly, sermons begin as a tiny "seed of life." They typically originate through real-life experiences that make a lot more sense when joined with the wisdom that is harnessed through daily, systematic Bible study. Through much thought and a great deal of prayer, the sermon begins to take on a life of its own. Until it is delivered, it grows inside you until you feel like you can't stand it any more. Finally, you deliver the sermon and your soul is relieved from the weight of that matter. Then the sermon takes on a life of its own in the hearts of those who hear it.

I was right in the middle of this spiritual birthing process when this book was born. My own sermon about the Year of Jubilee was about half developed in my spirit and my soul was just about ready to give birth to the teaching that had germinated and grown within my heart for a long, long time. But just as I was about to launch into some final intense preparations for that teaching, the

Holy Spirit spoke forcefully to my heart and said, "Wait a minute. Don't preach that sermon on the Year of Jubilee. I have something different I want you to do with the understanding I have given you regarding this matter."

Of course, I was perplexed by this change of course and more than a little frustrated. My heroes and mentors were preaching about Jubilee. My friends were preaching about Jubilee. I wanted to preach about Jubilee too, especially since I had a different "twist" on the subject. But God said, "No, I have something else I want you to do. I want you to write a book. I want you to keep studying until you connect a few more dots and then I want you to write down what you learn so you can help a lot more people better understand the eternal principles I sought to convey when I established the Year of Jubilee in the first place."

So I set aside my plans to preach a sermon on the subject and instead, I continued to study. Then one day, it all came together for me. On that memorable day, I was reading a passage of Scripture that is quite familiar to all of us. Certainly, it was familiar to me. You know, as I do, that familiar passages often lose their ability to impact us because we tend to speed right through them, focusing only upon the truths we have already gleaned from them, rarely slowing down to look for new nuggets or revelation that await our probing minds. But on this occasion, I broke with that bad habit and allowed God to show me something I think will help you. It certainly helped me.

What was the passage of Scripture that I was reading when all this happened? I was reading that familiar passage from Isaiah, the same passage that Jesus was asked to read when He revealed His identity as Messiah and when He announced His earthly ministry to the members of His hometown synagogue in Nazareth. I was reading Isaiah 61:1-2, which declares prophetically:

The Spirit of the Sovereign LORD is on me, because the LORD has anointed me to preach good news to the poor. He has sent me to bind up the brokenhearted, to proclaim freedom for the captives and release from darkness for the prisoners, to proclaim the year of the LORD's favor.

When I read this passage anew, something really came alive within me. The Holy Spirit was directing me to join the Lord in proclaiming the year of the Lord's favor. And, of course, I was excited to do so. To think that I would be announcing the same liberating truths that Jesus himself proclaimed during His earthly tenure was indeed exhilarating. But then I began to wonder: Which year are we talking about? Which year is "the year of the Lord's favor?" With my mind fixed firmly upon the Law of Moses and the Old Testament Year of Jubilee, I was intent on finding out when the next Jubilee would be on the modern calendar. If God was going to have a year of favor, I wanted to know exactly when to expect that year.

Of course, you have probably guessed already what I learned that day as I continued to pray, to study, and to lay this whole concept of favor before the Lord in an effort to gain His wisdom on the matter. What I learned is that every year is the year of God's favor, especially for those who no longer live under the Old Testament Law, but who live under the grace and truth of Jesus Christ.

At that moment, it became quite clear to me that my next assignment in ministry was to teach people how to recognize, accept, and live in the favor of God, a favor that God intends to bestow upon His people at all times. I knew that the Lord was calling me and directing me to help His people understand that they are favored and to learn how to appropriate His favor on a daily basis. I knew that He was calling me to explain to other believers that

His blessings are not confined to "special" days on the calendar. The things of God are no longer held at bay while we wait for the Year of Jubilee to arrive. Instead, God now intends for His people to enter His presence every day, not just on the Day of Atonement, and He intends for His people to walk in His favor every day, not just in the Year of Jubilee.

I hope this book will help you see what perhaps you have never seen before about God's thoughts toward you and His intentions in your life. I hope this book will fill you with the joy that comes only from knowing exactly where you stand with God, and I hope it will help fill you with the passion and excitement that comes only from an understanding of the type of life God intends for you to live, not in the future, but now; not in heaven, but here.

As you read this book, my prayer for you is that your mind will be stretched, your heart will be enlarged, and your faith will be expanded to both believe and receive all that God has for you in this life. If you can come to fully trust in the fact that you are highly favored by God, your whole life will change and so will your destiny.

-- Dr. Dave Martin

INTRODUCTION

THE GREATEST REWARD

I believe that favor is the greatest reward a person could ever receive from the Lord. Favor is better than money. While money cannot buy you favor, favor can definitely bring you money. Favor is better than fame. While fame cannot bring you God's favor, the favor of God can absolutely bring you respect from key individuals and cause you to stand out within large groups. Favor is better than life. In fact, King David wrote, "Thy lovingkindness is better than life" (Psalm 63:3, KJV).

Favor will determine the level of your income. Favor will deepen your important relationships and the friendships you forge as you associate with the right people. Favor will flood your life with joy, with happiness, with passion, and with a sense of purpose and significance. Favor will intensify your worship and enhance your intimacy with the Lord. Favor also will ward off the enemy and neutralize his relentless attacks against you. Favor will cause you to regain in a day what Satan has stolen from you over the years.

Just think about this for a few seconds. The Bible tells us that Satan has three "jobs" in this world. His jobs are "to steal, and to kill, and to destroy" (John 10:10, KJV) all that God has birthed in your life. So if you can think for a moment about those areas in your life that have "died," if you can think about those things and opportunities that your accuser has stolen from you, and if you can recount all the relationships and the innocence that the devil has destroyed in your life, you should take heart that God's favor is available to "restore to you the years that the locust hath eaten, the cankerworm, and the caterpiller, and the palmerworm" (Joel 2:25, KJV).

Favor can change a medical report. We see this in the Bible. Because Sarah was barren, she could not give Abraham the son that God had promised to him. As Sarah grew older and as the years accumulated, the possibilities for her to become a mother diminished with every passing day. Then finally, at the age of 90, when the medical reports merged with the physical realities of Sarah's age and it looked as if God's promise would go unfulfilled, the Bible tells us that "the LORD visited Sarah as he had said, and the LORD did unto Sarah as he had spoken. For Sarah conceived, and bare Abraham a son in his old age, at the set time of which God had spoken to him" (Genesis 21:1-2, KJV).

Favor is a seed that can be sown. The apostle Paul said, "Be not deceived; God is not mocked: for whatsoever a man soweth, that shall he also reap" (Galatians 6:7, KJV). So you have the ability to sow favor into the lives of others just as God has sown favor into your life, and you have a right to expect favor to come back into your life as the appropriate harvest for the favor you have sown. Favor, therefore, is reciprocal. It is part of the ongoing cycle of spiritual life.

Of course, whether we are talking about God's favor medically, relationally, financially, or spiritually, we cannot always expect a return on investment immediately. The farmer who sows seed and faithfully works that seed while it is in the ground has a perfect right to demand a return on his investment. He has a right to expect the seed to grow and produce crops. Likewise, the financier who sows his money into an investment portfolio and who patiently waits for those investments to mature has a perfect right to anticipate a return on his investment as well. He has a right to expect his money to grow and to produce more money. In time, the faithful man or faithful woman will always reap what they sow, and they will reap more than they sow. But they also will reap after they sow, so they may not reap right away. The reward comes after the effort. The prize comes after the race. The victory comes after the battle. And God's favor comes on the backside of faithfulness.

So never give up. The favor of God is there for you, and it can affect a major change in your life in a single moment of time. Your job as a believer is to keep believing and keep trusting God and keep doing what is right while you pray for God's favor. The favor of the Lord is your heritage as a child of God. It is your birthright, part of the richness and wealth of the Christian life. But like anything worthwhile, God's favor is sometimes delayed, and that is why you must persevere and never doubt its eventual manifestation in your life. Don't give up if the harvest you have worked for doesn't arrive today or tomorrow. Don't give up if it is delayed by new trials or by setbacks. Keep sowing good seed and keep asking God for new places to sow, for although "weeping may endure for a night... joy cometh in the morning" (Psalm 30:5, KJV). The favor of God is your promised reward.

Because I believe what I am telling you in this book, my wife Christine and I try to sow something every day ourselves. Why? Because we want to reap something every day! Sometimes we do and sometimes we don't, but we can say with certainty that we always eventually reap what we sow and we always eventually reap *more* than we sow. God is good, and He honors His Word. He showers His favor upon us in ways too numerous to recount. He enriches our lives in every way imaginable. We live in God's favor, and we enjoy God's favor. And, in response to God's favor on our lives, we look for more opportunities to sow favorably into the lives of others.

How can you sow favor in such a way as to perpetuate God's favor in your own life? Just look around you. Open your spiritual eyes and look for legitimate needs that you have the ability to meet. It doesn't take a lot of effort to meet financial needs, especially small ones. It doesn't take a lot of ingenuity to meet emotional needs, particularly the simple ones. It doesn't take a lot of work to meet needs for significance, acceptance, or encouragement. It doesn't take a lot of creativity to just roll up your sleeves and help someone move or finish that new addition to their house. So start sowing. Call forth the favor of God upon your life by sowing into the lives and work of others.

You can sow favor into your pastor and his wife. You can sow favor into your mentor or your teacher. You can sow favor into a neighbor or a coworker. You can even sow favor into your spouse, your children, or your parents. Just look around you. But unfortunately, most of us become spiritually blind. The necessary tasks of life and the urgency of the many responsibilities we bear often distract us to the point that we cannot see the basic human needs around us and the multiple opportunities God gives us every day to impact the lives of others and change the world. We are simply too preoccupied with living to live fully.

But for those who can open their eyes to see the needs around them and for those who can break out of their routines long enough to do something about those needs by sowing favor into those who are hurting, the work of God becomes easier and easier while it simultaneously becomes more rewarding. This is why Paul encourages us to "not become weary in doing good, for at the proper time we will reap a harvest if we do not give up. Therefore, as we have opportunity, let us do good to all people, especially to those who belong to the family of believers" (Galatians 6:9-10).

The Bible tells us that "Jesus grew in wisdom and stature, and in favor with God and men" (Luke 2:52). It is possible to increase in favor with God. It also is possible to increase in favor with men. It is possible to learn how to show more favor so we also can reap more favor. It is possible to start low and finish high, to start slowly and finish with strength. Favor is something we learn; it is not something that comes naturally to fallen man. But just as we grow in our ability to show favor *to* men and to reap favor *from* men, we also grow in our ability to receive favor from God. The favor of God is tightly knit to the favor we show others. As we become channels of His favor to others, He pours more favor into our lives. And that's the point: You should become a conduit of God's favor to those around you, but you also should expect, in return, a copious and constant outpouring of God's favor upon your life as a direct result of the favor you have shown to others.

My intention in the pages that follow is to teach you how to manifest favor while simultaneously encouraging you to expect favor in your own life. If you are doing what God wants you to do, you should start expecting God's favor to increase in your life, your home, your ministry, and your business. It's really a great arrangement. God wants you to take the focus off yourself and place it upon Him. As you place your focus on God, He will direct you to act upon that new focus by serving others in His name. Your focus, therefore, will move from yourself to others. In return, God will shift His attention to you. So as you're covering the backs of others, God is covering your back, and everybody is satisfied while the Lord is glorified. What an arrangement! What a plan!

You need to know right now that God has no limitations. So why do so many of God's people limit Him? The favor of God is without measure, so I want to encourage you to take the limits off God. Obviously, I cannot speak for you, but I am ready for God's unlimited favor in my life, and Christine, my wife, is ready for that as well. How about you? Are you ready to change your life and the way you live it? Are you ready to experience favor you cannot even imagine? So much favor that you can't keep track of everything that happens to you in a day?

This book will tell you a lot more about the principle of divine favor and how it is supposed to operate in your life. This book also will help you learn how to appropriate God's favor in your life on a daily basis. To start the conversation, however, let me share with you briefly how Christine and I began to recognize this divine quality in the Scriptures, how we learned to accept it as a reality for the modern Christian even though most of the Christian world seems oblivious to its existence, and how we have learned to walk under the mantle of divine favor that God has placed on our lives and ministry. Although I don't fully understand it and even though I can't fully explain it, God has shown the two of us the most incredible grace and miraculous power over the years. His favor has been undeniable in our lives. Now, He has launched us into a new season in our lives and ministry, where He seems to use us regularly to spread the favor around. It seems like everywhere we go, the people we meet begin to experience an increase in favor and in their own understanding of it and how it should operate in their lives.

It all began in 1997, when we heard a life-changing sermon by Dr. Oral Roberts. His teaching, based on Deuteronomy 1:11, described the favor that God had for the people of Israel, even though they were often more of a problem for God than a blessing. While expounding some of the difficulties he had endured as the leader of God's people, Moses nevertheless said to the Israelites, "May the LORD, the God of your fathers, increase you a thousand times and bless you as he has promised" (Deuteronomy 1:11).

When we heard this teaching on this little verse, Christine and I could not believe that we had never really noticed this verse before. We had read the Bible multiple times, and we had read Deuteronomy just as many times. But somehow, that powerful little verse had never really impacted us or stayed with us until a godly messenger helped us see its significance. Dr. Roberts' point that day was that God will give His people a thousand times more of anything that they need as they attempt to live for Him: more joy, more wisdom, more health, more peace, more miracles, more money, more love, more anointing, more power, more victories, and more favor! If we walk in faithfulness and if we walk in the shadow of the Almighty, we can have a thousand times more favor in our lives than we ever thought we could.

Immediately after hearing this teaching, my heart was stirred and forever changed because my spiritual eyes had been opened to a new reality, a new truth. I said to Christine, "We have to sow a seed for a thousand times more favor to begin flowing in our lives." (You can tell that I believe in activating the promises of God in my life by sowing some sort of spiritual seed.) So Christine let me know that she and I were on the same page in this matter, and we began to ask God what kind of "seed" we should sow.

Obviously, a financial "seed" is the most practical seed to sow and the first thing that comes to mind, so I thought about giving a special offering of $1,000 to represent the thousand times additional favor we were expecting in our lives. But when we opened our checkbook to prepare that "seed," we discovered that we didn't have $1,000 and probably couldn't get it any time soon. I was deeply disappointed, although I think the Lord was honored by my intentions. So I asked the Lord, "What should we do?" I prayed and let Him know that the truth revealed to me through His Word had changed my life, and, as the spiritual head of my home, I wanted to lead my family in an act of obedience and faith that could open the floodgates of His incredible favor upon our lives.

That's when God spoke to me, directing me to give $111 as a symbolic representation of my confidence in the promise of Deuteronomy 1:11. When God spoke that directive to my heart, I said, "Okay, I can do that." But I actually ended up writing three checks totaling $333: $111 for me, $111 for Christine, and $111 for our ministry, which we had recently launched. In the pages that follow, you will hear a few of the many testimonies regarding the favor God began to show us in response to that single act of obedience but at this point, I want to share the first of those testimonies with you, one that I think will serve as a good illustration of God's desire to lavish favor upon His people. This simple demonstration of divine favor seemed to open the floodgates to a new lifestyle for us and served as the springboard for many blessings that would follow.

Less than two weeks after we had sown this $333 seed, a lady was visiting our house. While she was there, she told Christine and me that the Holy Spirit had spoken to her and had told her that she should buy us something for our house. She asked us what we needed, and I told her that there was a particular bed we had been admiring for our bedroom. She told us that she wanted to buy that bed for us.

One month later, we received another unexpected blessing that made us realize that God's favor is manifested in more than material and financial ways. We had been praying for Christine's grandfather to give his heart to the Lord. At the time, he was 74 years old, and we knew that statistics were not in our favor. As people grow older, they become statistically less likely to accept Christ as their Savior, so we knew that we needed a real miracle. And we got it! Grandpa Olsen lifted his hand in response to an altar call at a church in Sarasota, Florida, that night. Praise the Lord for His unmerited favor! Praise Him a thousand times over for His goodness and His love!

I know that you need increase in your life just as Christine and I needed it in our lives, both materially and spiritually. You have a God-given desire deep inside of you for a better life, a better walk with the Lord, better progress toward your appointed purpose, better relationships, better results, and more success. Because the Spirit of God dwells within you, you cannot simply "settle" for what you have and where you are. The same God who created you and who saved you has given you a soul that passionately desires increase, growth, and excellence in every area of life. The God whose first words to Adam were, "Be fruitful and increase in number; fill the earth and subdue it" (Genesis 1:28), is the same God who wants you to "be fruitful and increase in number; fill the earth and subdue it." God doesn't want to withhold any good thing from you. Rather, He wants to overload you with His benefits. Day by day, week by week, month by month, and year by year, He wants to set you free from the things that limit you and pour good things into your life in greater abundance. A thousand times greater!

There are many Christians living in the land of "not enough," "barely enough," and "never enough" while God wants us living in the land of "more than enough." God wants to show favor to all His children, including you, so I truly hope that this biblical promise is getting into your heart and your mind. When it does, a new day will dawn for you in your spiritual life. Your relationship with God will intensify, your expectations of God will rise, and your esteem for God's abilities will increase. Like Christine and me, you will never be the same. And regardless of how far you have come in your Christian walk, you will ascend to experiential heights that are a thousand times more than anything you have known in the past. A day of favor will change your life forever.

Actually, I like the way the man phrased it when he preached the sermon that changed my life. He said, "A day of favor is worth a thousand days of labor." Ain't that the truth! You can't work enough to get everything you want from God. You can't work enough hours or perform enough good deeds to get everything you want from the Lord. But when you have the favor of the Lord upon your life, things that were once out of reach become quite attainable and things that seemed to constantly elude you start flowing miraculously toward you. Favor will cause you to rise to the top.

Before we get to the meat and potatoes of this book, let's take a brief look at the life of one of God's most favored servants. I'm talking about Joseph, whose life story is found in the book of Genesis. You know the story of his life. When Joseph was just a young man, his father gave him a coat. But this wasn't just any coat. This was a special coat, a coat of many colors. The coat signified Joseph's special place in his father's heart. Joseph, because he was young and naïve, showed off his beautiful coat to everyone, including his eleven brothers.

Of course, Joseph didn't know at that young age what many mature believers have learned. Joseph didn't know that, due to the power of jealousy and envy, it is not always wise to advertise your favor. It can be dangerous to flaunt the blessings of God. In his ignorance, therefore, Joseph showed his brothers the wonderful new coat that Jacob had given to him, hoping that they would share his joy and excitement. But by showing them his coat, Joseph was basically saying to them, "Look at the coat Dad gave me. It's my coat of favor, my special coat of unconditional approval. Our father has elevated me above the rest of you." So Joseph's brothers, his own flesh and blood, became jealous. They took the coat off him, beat him, and threw him into a pit. Then they pulled him out of the pit and sold him to slave traders, who took him to Egypt. There he suffered for two decades as a slave and a prisoner. Nevertheless, God was with Joseph.

Now I know what you're thinking. You're thinking, "That doesn't sound like favor to me, and, if it is favor, I don't want any part of that." There are two things you should know, however. First of all, most of Joseph's suffering wasn't due to God's favor as much as it was due to Joseph's foolishness. You just shouldn't cast your pearls before swine. The Bible warns us that to do so is to invite those who don't understand your pearls to trample them underfoot. So be careful how you share the details of God's blessings, and be careful with whom you share that information. Only share your dreams and blessings with those who can appreciate them and applaud them. Never share them with people who might misunderstand them or be envious of them.

Second, never think that a life of favor is a life devoid of suffering. Suffering is part of the Christian life, and favor doesn't change that reality. Jesus and most of the writers of the New Testament taught a lot about suffering and about its role in spiritual growth.

Even though God's favor won't eliminate suffering from your life, it certainly will help you rise above the suffering and combat the natural human tendency to become bitter in the face of suffering or succumb to self pity. So while having favor in your life won't keep you from having problems, it can keep your problems from having you. It can help you rise above them, just as Joseph managed to do, and it can help you triumph in spite of them. Regardless of the way things must have looked through his prison bars, Joseph still managed to achieve his dreams because he never allowed his circumstances to define him or to blind him to the presence of God's favor in his life.

While Joseph was a slave in Potiphar's house, for instance, the favor of God was still evidently upon him. Potiphar himself recognized it and eventually came to trust Joseph completely. He basically handed Joseph the keys to the car, the checkbook, all the credit cards, and the password to the household computer, saying, "You run this place." And the Bible tells us that Potiphar's house was blessed because Joseph was in charge:

> *The LORD was with Joseph and he prospered, and he lived in the house of his Egyptian master. When his master saw that the LORD was with him and that the LORD gave him success in everything he did, Joseph found favor in his eyes and became his attendant. Potiphar put him in charge of his household, and he entrusted to his care everything he owned. From the time he put him in charge of his household and of all that he owned, the*

LORD blessed the household of the Egyptian because of Joseph. The blessing of the LORD was on everything Potiphar had, both in the house and in the field (Genesis 39:2-5).

When you really come to understand the favor of God and how it works in your life, you will know that favor is contagious. The favor that is upon my life is often manifested in the lives of those around me, and the favor that God desires to pour upon you will also affect those around you when you learn to embrace it and allow it to do its eternal work in your life. Like Abraham, you are blessed to be a blessing. Joseph, who was Abraham's great-grandson, understood this spiritual principle.

Eventually, however, more trouble came Joseph's way because Potiphar's wife accused him of sexual assault and Joseph ended up in prison. But regardless of how things might have looked at that low moment, God's favor had not been withdrawn from Joseph's life. In fact, it increased to meet the need of the moment, and the Bible tells us that the warden started putting Joseph in charge of the prison. Just as it was in Potiphar's house, so it was in the prison. The blessings of God began to flow and the favor of God began to manifest. In fact, God's favor began to flow so noticeably that the captain of the prison guard stopped worrying about things and just released them to Joseph's care. Once again, Joseph had risen to the top, not through his own efforts, but as a result of God's favor upon his life.

Joseph's master took him and put him in prison, the place where the king's prisoners were confined. But while Joseph was there in the prison, the LORD was with him; he showed him kindness and granted him favor in the eyes of the prison warden. So the warden put Joseph in charge of all those held in the prison, and

he was made responsible for all that was done there. The war-
den paid no attention to anything under Joseph's care, because the
LORD was with Joseph and gave him success in whatever he did
(Genesis 39:20-23).

While Joseph was in prison, God was showing favor to Joseph in another way, a providential way that could not be seen with the naked eye, because God was working behind the scenes to fulfill the vision He had given to Joseph as a young man. Eventually, the time came for that vision to be realized, so God arranged circumstances so Joseph could interpret a dream for Pharaoh, the king of Egypt. As a result, Pharaoh also recognized the favor of God upon Joseph's life and God used Pharaoh to elevate Joseph to his destiny in a single day. At Pharaoh's command, Joseph was moved from the prison to the palace in a matter of 24 hours. His status was changed from that of a convicted felon to second-in-command in the world's mightiest kingdom. All in one short day!

Then Pharaoh said to Joseph, "Since God has made all this known
to you, there is no one so discerning and wise as you. You shall be
in charge of my palace, and all my people are to submit to your
orders. Only with respect to the throne will I be greater than you."
So Pharaoh said to Joseph, "I hereby put you in charge of the whole
land of Egypt." Then Pharaoh took his signet ring from his fin-
ger and put it on Joseph's finger. He dressed him in robes of fine
linen and put a gold chain around his neck. He had him ride
in a chariot as his second-in-command, and men shouted before
him, "Make way!" Thus he put him in charge of the whole land of
Egypt (Genesis 41:39-43).

Favor will accelerate your destiny in life. Things that may have developed in the past for you over many years will only take a year when they are seasoned with God's favor. The things that once took you a year to do will now take a matter of weeks or days. The days that came "hard" will now come "easy." In fact, with God's favor upon your life, your entire world could change before you go to bed tonight. It happened to Joseph and it has happened to me. It could happen to you, too. Joseph was in prison one day. The next day, he was in the palace. In a matter of hours, his life had totally changed and his destiny had been realized. He woke up that morning in a prison cell with a guard outside his door, and he laid down that night on a satin pillow in a royal residence with a personal attendant outside his door. Only God could do that for Joseph. But God is no respecter of persons. He wants to do that for you, as well.

I want you to stop whatever you are doing. I want you to put a few things on hold that may be taking up your time right now. Instead, I want you to sit down and read this book. *The Force of Favor* is not a lengthy book, so you can read it in a relatively short time. Nevertheless, it is filled with revelations concerning a truth that can change your life forever, the truth about God's loving favor toward His children and His desire to show that favor in many and varied ways. If you can find the time to absorb this revelation and find the faith to apply it to your life, I know that the doctrine of divine favor can change your life forever, just as it changed mine. I want you to realize that you are blessed and highly favored of the Lord, and I want you to learn to expect God's blessings every day and walk in the assurance that they belong to you every moment of your earthly life.

You are God's favored!

CHAPTER 1
DECLARING FAVOR

GOD'S FAVOR IS ACTIVATED
BY YOUR CONFESSION

While most books seem to save the strongest chapter for the back of the book, I want to start my book with what is perhaps the most formidable chapter. From the outset, I want to share with you what I consider the most important thing you can do when it comes to appropriating God's favor for your life. The rest of this book will fill in some of the gaps, answer some of your questions, and expound on the principles I will lay out for you in this opening chapter.

I want to start this process by telling you about the importance of confessing God's favor and declaring God's favor over your life. Before I get to the subject of favor, however, I need to share with you a little something from a biblical perspective regarding the importance of confession in the Christian life. The word *confess* comes from a Latin word which basically means "to agree with" or "to say the same thing." When you confess a crime on a witness stand in a courtroom, therefore, you are pretty much agreeing with your accusers. When you confess your sins to God during a prayer of repentance, you are basically saying the same thing about yourself that God has said already. God said in His written Word that "all have sinned, and come short of the glory of God" (Romans3:23, KJV), so you are saying the same thing about yourself when you confess your sins. You are agreeing with God.

The spiritual practice of verbal confession is a lot more than just a hocus-pocus approach to life. Declaring a biblical truth out loud with your mouth is a spiritual exercise of agreement with divine truth. I know that some people get weird about this. They believe they can bring all kinds of evil down upon their heads with a slight slip of the tongue or that every careless word will come true for them in a negative way. I don't believe that, but I do believe that the constant repetitions of our mouths reveal what is inside us. I believe that they also shape what is inside us. Jesus said, "Out of the abundance of the heart the mouth speaketh" (Matthew 12:34, KJV). What comes out of the mouth reflects what is inside a man's heart. It is also true that, eventually, if we start deliberately saying those things that we know to be true, the inverse can happen, and those confessions can shape what is on the inside, particularly when those confessions are based on truth, not fantasy.

To say the same thing verbally that God has already said about you in the Bible is not fantasy or an exercise in vanity. It is a powerful act of faith that can activate the presence and promises of God in your life, because, if you say it loud enough and often enough, it will finally begin to seep into your heart and mind, affecting the way you think, the way you feel, the way you perceive the world, and the way you live your life. Then the things that come out of your mouth will start flowing from experience rather than beginning faith. Your words will have power. They will pack a punch. And they will truly reshape your life and the lives of those around you.

I truly believe in the power of confession. I believe in declaring "the wonderful works of God" (Acts 2:11, KJV). I believe that if I will repeat those wonderful works out loud because I believe them, I will begin to actually see them manifested in my life. I will certainly begin to see positive changes in my attitudes, perceptions, and behaviors, and that can never be a bad thing.

The words of your mouth (your confessions) are powerful. They reflect what you believe, and what you believe shapes your life. When you declare things, therefore, you should be careful with whom you are agreeing. Are you confessing (saying) the same thing about yourself that the world is saying about you? Are you confessing (saying) the same thing about yourself that the devil is saying about you? Or are you confessing (saying) the same thing about yourself that God is saying about you?

King Solomon noted that, "death and life are in the power of the tongue" (Proverbs 18:21, KJV). You have to learn to declare, to confess, and to say the same things out loud that God has said about you in His Word. This is especially true when it comes to favor. In both explicit and implicit ways, the Bible makes it clear that the people of God are especially loved and that they are highly regarded by the Lord. He watches over His children. He protects them, guides them, corrects them, and blesses them. God the Father favors those who are His own, and the Bible is replete with references affirming this point. As children of God, therefore, we should learn to agree with God and what He has said about us in His Word. We should learn to say the same things about ourselves that God has said. Consequently, I like to walk around saying these things. I like to repeat verbally the blessings that God has promised to me as His child and declare with my mouth the favor that my God desires to show to me. In fact, there are seven specific aspects of life that motivate me to pause in order to express God's favor in those vital areas.

FAVOR FOR MY FAMILY

Nothing in life is more important than your relationships, and none of your relationships are more important than those which exist within your family. The dynamics that exist between husbands and wives and the dynamics that are ongoing between parents and children are difficult sometimes, and they require a great deal of grace from above and attention from below. You know, as I do, that family life can be the most rewarding part of life or the most painful. There is no in-between. Consequently, if there is any place where we need the constant favor of God, it is in our homes and within our families.

Favor has saved many marriages. Favor has healed many wounds. Favor has restored many relationships and made right many situations. Divine favor is the salve and the ointment of the home, the lubricant that makes all the parts work together without friction. For this reason, I frequently pronounce God's favor over my family. Of course, I ask for God's favor in my own life, too. But I really focus on declaring His favor over my wife and my son. Whenever I encounter situations within my home that frustrate me or leave me bewildered, I just release those situations to the Lord and, as I remind Him of my position as spiritual head of my home, I declare His favor over the situation at hand. I refuse to accept any negative circumstance in my home, and I refuse to settle for second best in my family life. I also refuse to surrender my family to Satan or to the world. I take charge of that which confronts us as a family by releasing God, through my verbal confessions, to do good and mighty things to guide us, protect us, preserve us, unite us, and enable us to show grace one to another. I won't allow a foreign spirit to invade our lives without placing a hedge of protection around my home through the confession of God's Word. I declare His favor.

Drive away doubt and fear by saying the same thing about your most important relationships that God has said about them already. Declare that your wife loves you and that you love your wife. Declare that your children will follow the Lord and that the Lord will be with them day by day in their personal lives. If any members of your family are unsaved, declare that the favor of God will intrude upon their lives so the devil's grip on their minds can be broken. Declare that God will use you in some way as His instrument of grace to help direct your family members toward Him. Declare that He will control circumstances, direct events, connect people with opportunities, and bring pressure to bear through a direct witness of His Spirit until your loved ones surrender their hearts and lives to the Lord.

Speak it. Believe it. Watch it happen right in front of your face as you say the same thing out loud about your family that God has said to you quietly in the privacy of your own heart. By declaring God's favor over your children as they sleep at night, you can be assured that God will watch over them with a jealousy that cannot be explained or equaled. By declaring God's favor over special family events and your precious times together, you can be assured that God will use those occasions to create lasting memories and to draw you closer as a family unit.

God's favor is there for you and your family. Activate it by speaking God's favor over your family and home.

FAVOR IN YOUR WORK

Next to your relationships, there is nothing more important in this earthly life than your work. Your work brings you either frustration or satisfaction. It brings you either bounty or lack. It brings you ei-

35

ther purpose and significance or indifference and aimlessness. It becomes a meaningful indicator of who you are, and the type of work you do and the way you do it becomes a legacy that endures beyond your lifetime.

You need the favor of God in your work and on your job, because your work will determine your level of personal satisfaction with life and your job will determine your income. So don't hesitate to pronounce God's blessing on your employment and upon all your business operations. Every morning, when you pull into the parking lot to go to work, declare God's favor over your day, over your labor, and over all your professional relationships and interactions. Declare God's favor with your boss, because your boss has the power to increase your salary or promote you to a higher position. In fact, before you even accept a new job, declare God's favor over your job search. Say the same thing that God has already said about you when He declared, "I know the plans I have for you… plans to prosper you and not to harm you, plans to give you hope and a future" (Jeremiah 29:11).

When some people go to a job interview, their confessions are quite negative, whether those confessions are muttered out loud or whether they are repeated quietly within the mind of the one who believes them. These people tell themselves, "I can't get this job. I don't even know why I'm here. I'm under-qualified. I don't have enough experience. I probably won't get hired." Then when they finally do get hired somewhere, they often tell themselves, "I can't do this. I'm faking it. I'm not very good at what I do. Besides, this is a dead-end job anyway, so why should I care?" If you don't believe these confessions have a direct bearing on the outcome of people's lives, then you need a wakeup call, because the way we view life has a lot more impact on the direction of our lives than you might think.

For this reason and because you profess to be a follower of Christ, you need a different outlook, a different perspective, and a different approach to the way you are living. You need to start seeing things through the same pair of glasses that God puts on when He looks at your life, and you need to see the potential God brings to the table for you. You need to start saying the same things about yourself that God is saying about you and whispering to your heart. You need to go into your job interviews with a different belief system and a different attitude, and you need to say, "I am God's favorite. He loves me, and He has prepared me for this moment. I know this job might seem a little bit above me, but God has prepared me for it and He is getting ready to elevate me to the position He carved out for me long before this day. Therefore, I will get this job. I declare God's favor over my interview, that He might give me clarity of thought and communication. I declare God's favor over my conversations, that I might impress those who meet me. I declare God's favor over the environment and atmosphere, that there might be a real connection that will be evident to everyone involved. And I confess a spirit of excellence upon my life so that those who meet me will pick up on it and realize that I can do all things well, like Jesus."

Remember, as a child of God, "You will be blessed in the city and blessed in the country. The fruit of your womb will be blessed, and the crops of your land and the young of your livestock--the calves of your herds and the lambs of your flocks. Your basket and your kneading trough will be blessed. You will be blessed when you come in and blessed when you go out. The LORD will grant that the enemies who rise up against you will be defeated before you. They will come at you from one direction but flee from you in seven. The LORD will send a blessing on your barns and on everything you put your hand to" (Deuteronomy 28:3-8). And since so many of

God's blessings have to do with productivity, fruitfulness, and legacy, understand that these things come primarily through one's labors. Your job, therefore, is important to God, and your work is one of the most important reflections of your Christian testimony. Say the same things that God has said already about your work and your success in business.

FAVOR IN YOUR DEALINGS WITH PEOPLE

A large portion of the New Testament deals with the practicalities of getting along with other people. As Christians, we sometimes forget that relationships, though rewarding, can be difficult. Relationships demand mercy, patience, and grace. They demand gentleness, kindness, and love. This is why Paul could write a letter to a church filled with fallible people and still refer to them as "saints." This is why he could extol the virtues of the believers' faith in the opening chapter of his letter, then spend the next several pages rebuking them for the way they treat each other and instructing them regarding proper behavior toward those inside and outside the church.

In this life, you are going to have to deal with people, and you are going to have to deal with them on multiple levels. I have already mentioned those all-important relationships within your family, and I already have alluded to the important relationship you will have with your boss. Whether you like it or not, you are going to have close relationships and daily associations with a lot of people, including neighbors, coworkers, clients, and the friends of those you love. This includes your in-laws. You need God's favor in a big way when it comes to your dealings with people in life and in the marketplace.

If you own a business, you need favor with those people in your community who need your products and services. There probably are a lot of places these people can go to buy what you provide, but if you have favor with them, they will buy from you and they will remain loyal to you as good customers or clients. If you work for someone else, you probably either work in an office or "out in the field" with company accounts. If you work with accounts, you have to form relationships with the key decision-makers in other firms. You have to win them over as you earn their trust and respect. You have to compete on a daily basis with other salespeople who are calling on these decision-makers and offering them everything but the kitchen sink to switch over their business. You need favor. And if you work in an office or a factory, you have to learn to get along with the people beside you because those people, with all their idiosyncrasies, will probably still be working there tomorrow and the next day and the next.

So declare God's favor over your dealings with people and the relationships you forge in the marketplace. If you work for yourself, declare the favor of both God and man over your life (see Luke 2:52). If you work for someone else, declare God's favor over the work that you do and the relationships that are key to your success. If you own a store or business, declare God's favor over the industry that provides you with a living and over the public's perception of you. Declare God's favor with your clients and prospective clients, with your employees and peers, with your suppliers and delivery people, and with all those who will be interacting with you in some important way. If you are in the market to purchase a new home or car, declare God's favor over your efforts. If you are in the middle of efforts to downsize, declare God's favor in selling your home or your business. In all your dealings in the marketplace, confess that you will get the best deal possible and that people will quickly and willingly give you their very best and all the little "breaks" you can handle.

Also, don't overlook declaring God's favor with your children's teachers, those who provide lawn care, pest control services, and other work for you around your private residence, and even your neighbors. Yes, your neighbors! Believe it or not, they wield a lot of power over your life. Because of their demeanor toward you, they can either enrich your life greatly or make it terribly painful. You can't typically pick your neighbors and you certainly can't control them, but you can walk in favor with them if you will grasp God's provision of favor in that area and apply it to your life by believing it and confessing it.

I frequently declare God's favor over my neighborhood and my neighbors. As a result, I receive a lot of God's favor through their hands. I remember one night, several years ago, when Christine and I returned home after an exhausting ministry trip of more than two weeks. I love my work, and there is nothing my wife and I would rather be doing than ministry. We are grateful to God for the opportunity to pour into people's lives and help shape their destinies. Nevertheless, ministry can be exhausting and nothing is more physically depleting than travel. When we return home from an extended trip, therefore, we usually just collapse for a few days until we slowly start feeling the life creeping back into our worn-out bodies.

That's the way it was on this particular occasion when we pulled into our driveway shortly after sunset. As we were walking from our car to the front door of our house, we happened to notice our next-door neighbors, who were grilling chicken on the patio in preparation for their evening meal. We waved at them, then, in spite of being tired, we took a moment to walk next door to greet them. They politely asked about our trip, and we politely asked them about some things that were going on in their lives at that time. Then, without thinking much more about it, we made our way to our own front door, carried our luggage inside, and started the not-so-fun process of unpacking.

A few minutes later, there was a knock at our door. Who could that be? As I opened the door, I was surprised to see our neighbors standing on our back porch with a large platter of grilled chicken and vegetables. Christine and I had just been talking about dinner. We were too tired to cook. We were even too tired to get back in the car and drive to a restaurant. God knew exactly what we needed at that moment, and He provided for our needs through the hands of our neighbors. Why? Because He had given us favor with our neighbors! And why would our neighbors favor us? Because we had constantly declared God's favor over our relationships with them!

Realize that the people around you—from the teller at the bank to the guy at the drive-through window, from the receptionist at the front desk to the customer service agent on the other end of the line—can either make your life easier or make it really painful. And since the nurturing of relationships on all levels takes hard work, to say the least, also realize that you need God's favor in all your associations. You need His favor with your bank. You need His favor with city and county government leaders. You need His favor with your homeowners' association. You need His favor with your auto mechanic, your postal delivery person, and even the guy who presses your shirts and slacks.

How do you acquire this favor? Obviously, you have to do something. You have to work at nurturing an appropriate relationship with each of the people who impact your life directly and indirectly. You also have to apply the Christian graces of patience, love, mercy, and kindness in your dealings with people. I believe that all these processes begin with confession. Until you can say it, you don't really believe it. And when you start saying it, you will start living it. So declare God's favor over all your dealings with mankind.

FAVOR FOR YOUR HEALTH

There's an interesting little verse in the third epistle of St. John. I call this verse "interesting" because it invokes a "wish" upon God's people rather than a prayer. In this verse, John writes to the people of God, "Beloved, I wish above all things that thou mayest prosper and be in health, even as thy soul prospereth" (III John 2, KJV). Throughout most of the New Testament, we read prayers when one of the writers of Scripture wants to convey his deepest spiritual desires for the people to whom he is writing. In this verse, however, there is no prayer to God. Rather, there is a statement of hope or blessing—a declaration, if you will—that God's people might prosper and live healthy lives.

This verse should serve as our inspiration, as well as our guide, when it comes to the declaration of favor over our individual health and the health of those we love. If John, writing under the inspiration of the Holy Spirit, could pronounce favorable health upon the readers of his letter, then you and I have a right to pronounce the same blessing over ourselves and others. We can declare God's protection and health upon our children. We can declare God's health upon our husbands and wives. We can declare God's shield of good health around our homes and our places of business. We can declare God's health for our friends, work associates, and others who fall under the venue of our watchful eye.

Even though sickness is a natural consequence of living in this world, it doesn't have to be the accepted lifestyle of the believer. Yes, there are viruses and bacteria out there that can brutally assault the human body. Yes, we wear down our bodies when the stress in our lives goes up or our quality of sleep goes down. And yes, small children have to build immunity against deadly diseases by dealing with those things in kindergarten and elementary school. But that doesn't mean that the people of God have to live under the threat of sickness or accept sickness as a constant in their lives: "Moses was a hundred and twenty years old when he died, yet his eyes were not weak nor his strength gone" (Deuteronomy 34:7). John proved to us with his pronouncement of blessing that it is God's perfect will for His people to live healthy and pain-free lives.

So begin pronouncing God's blessings of divine health upon yourself and all those who are part of your life, especially those to whom you are responsible in one way or another. Pray for them, too, but always be sure to declare the favor of God upon their health and vitality.

FAVOR IN YOUR FINANCES

John made it clear that God wants us to prosper in health and in our souls, but most biblical references dealing with prosperity mention financial prosperity. In fact, the Bible has a lot more to say about money than you might imagine. The Old Testament is replete with promises dealing with financial abundance, increase, multiplication, and security. And at least one researcher has determined that money was the second most frequently mentioned subject in Jesus' ministry. Love was first.

So God isn't offended by money. In fact, He has a lot of nice things to say about money. For instance, God knows that "money answereth all things" (Ecclesiastes 10:19, KJV). In other words, money can solve a lot of problems. It can give you a lifestyle you can truly enjoy. It can eliminate a lot of worry and stress. It can improve the quality of your life all the way around, including your health. It can even give you more time with your family and the other important people in your life. Money is a really good thing as long as you keep it in perspective and make sure it is serving you (not the other way around).

Consequently, it is important to confess what you believe and to say out loud what you hold true. It is important to declare the goodness of God in the area of your finances. Obviously, saying something won't make it happen until you also act upon the thing you confess. But by saying something, you give birth to its reality in your life. By declaring God's favor over your finances, for instance, you create within your own heart a deeper respect for money. By declaring God's favor over your finances, you stir up a longing to become a better manager of the resources you currently have and you reprogram your thoughts so you can start the process of becoming more willing to do what is necessary to improve your future earning power. By declaring God's favor over your finances, you begin to realize that it is the Lord who gives you the ability to get wealth and that He is the source of your means.

Declare God's favor over your job, so you can earn more for your employer and for yourself. Declare God's favor over your bills, so the devourer won't consume all you make and the holes in the bottom of your bucket can be plugged. Declare God's favor over your tithes and offerings, so your church might use them to do great things for God and so you might be blessed as a result of releasing them to the Lord. Declare God's favor over your savings and investments, over your income-producing properties, over your long-range financial plans, and over new business ventures you may be launching. With God's favor and blessing, these things can produce more than you have a right to expect. Without His favor and blessing, these things can become just another dry well that yields nothing in exchange for your hard work and sacrifice.

FAVOR WHEN YOU TRAVEL

This one is especially near and dear to my heart, because I spend the majority of my life on the road, preaching in churches and teaching in schools and at various corporations and conferences around the world. I am constantly flying on airplanes, driving on unfamiliar roadways, meeting new people, and walking innocently into situations I could never have foreseen and for which I am often unprepared. I believe in traveling mercies and in the favor of God for those who are away from home.

Whenever I arrive in a new city or at a church where I will be ministering to the people on the Lord's behalf, I always declare favor with those people and with the purposes of God for that time and place. I always ask God to show me favor with all those I will encounter and to help me teach His people how they, too, can walk in the favor of God. It is exciting to live every day in the expectation of good things happening, not only at those destinations to which I am traveling, but also along the way. Travel can be boring, dangerous, and exhausting, so it is uplifting, to say the least, to see God's hand upon me as I wave goodbye to my family in order to pursue the mission He has given me to fulfill or to witness God's active intervention in our lives as Christine, Solomon and I glance over our shoulders at our disappearing house when we depart for the airport to travel to another unfamiliar location so we can live out of a suitcase and eat our meals at chain restaurants.

I remember one time when Christine and I had wrapped up several days of meetings in the Seattle area. We were scheduled to return to Dallas (our home at that time) the next morning, when I discovered that there was a flight leaving at 11:50 that night. We were really anxious to get home, so we decided we would try to change our itinerary and catch that late flight. I called the airline to find out the availability of seats on that particular flight only to learn that the flight was already full. Besides, there would be a $150 upcharge for the two of us to change our flight plans, because we would actually be changing the day for our return flight by a whole 10 minutes. In spite of the bad report, however, Christine and I packed our bags and headed for the airport. On the way, we presented our situation to the Lord, asked for His divine intervention, and declared His favor over the circumstances. We joined hands and thanked God, because somehow we just knew that we would be flying out that night.

When we arrived at the airport to change our tickets, the woman behind the counter reminded us that the flight was full. She told us we could put our names on the standby list, but she was not very encouraging. There were six names on the list ahead of ours. We journeyed to the gate anyway and we waited. Eventually, they began loading the plane, but we just continued to declare the favor of God over the situation. Then, after a few minutes, they began to call those who had placed their names on the standby list. They called the first few names quickly, then a long time passed before they called the next couple of names. We sat there, knowing we had declared God's favor upon this trip, but the time seemed to pass very slowly as we patiently waited for God to manifest what we had proclaimed in faith.

Eventually, a man came off the plane and spoke with the agent behind the counter. We clearly heard him say that there were only two seats left on the plane, and he instructed the agent to go ahead and fill those last two seats. Of course, the last two seats were for Christine and me. They called us to the counter to make us aware that we had been selected to fill the last two seats on the flight. They also called us to the counter to offer us an apology. Due to the fact that the flight was full, they would have to put us in First Class. To make this change more palatable, however, they would waive the $150 upcharge to accommodate us for any inconvenience. Have you ever traveled in First Class? For years, I used to wonder what happened up there when they closed that little curtain. Now I know. We had real silverware, all the food and drinks we could handle, and the food was hot for a change. A little bit of heaven on earth and a real blessing for us at the end of a long, hard week of work!

This is just one example of the blessings we have received as we have learned to declare God's favor in the different situations we encounter while we are away from home, doing the work that God has called us to do. I share these real-life accounts with you, not to boast, but to encourage you to do the same thing when you travel. Declare God's goodness and favor over your life, your health, your energy, your finances, your time, your meetings, your work, your travel plans, your accommodations, your food, and everything else that will be a vital part of getting you from here to there and back again. If you are traveling for pleasure instead of work, declare God's favor over the services you will receive, over the creation of many wonderful memories, over the weather, and over a perfect balance between rest and excitement while you are away from home. In brief, expect good things to happen to you.

Many times in my life, I have received God's favor without declaring it, confessing it, or even recognizing it. But since learning the principle of declaring God's promises before I realize them, I have noticed a significant increase in the frequency and intensity of God's blessings upon my life. The force of favor is an incredible benefit all of us have as children of God.

FAVOR IN EVERYDAY LIFE

Everyday life extracts a lot from us. In the course of a day, you will run a lot more errands and encounter a lot more people than you might imagine. You will spend a lot of money, make a lot of decisions, drive a lot of miles, and consume a lot of time just taking care of yourself, your home, and your family, not to mention your professional responsibilities. You need God's favor in everyday life, so you should start declaring His favor over everything, even the little things that you do every day.

I remember an occasion recently when I needed to run to the store to get something. I was in a hurry, but I really had no choice. I had to go, so on the way, I declared God's favor over my little mission. I declared His favor in the parking lot, and I found an unlikely space to park that was near the front entrance to the store. Then, once inside, I declared His favor over my search, which was quickly successful. And finally, I declared His favor as I approached the checkout line to pay for the item I was purchasing.

Of course, you guessed it: The checkout line was long and there was only one clerk ringing a register. To make things worse, the lady in the front of the line wanted to write a check. But I just declared God's favor and prayed quietly under my breath, "Lord, You know I'm in a hurry tonight, and it's not my fault. Could You show me favor by opening a new checkout line? People are waiting for me, and this is important." Just seconds after praying that prayer and declaring God's favor in the situation, a man walked by and said to me as he approached the next register, "Sir, I'll take you over here." God's favor was once again demonstrated in my life as a direct result of my faithful declaration of His promises.

It doesn't matter how big your problem might be or how small. If it is a legitimate need, God is concerned, and God wants to become involved in your life by showing you that you are indeed His favorite. He has elevated you above those who do not know Him, in the same way that an earthly father elevates his own children above the children of neighbors and friends. As an earthly father might show respect toward all people yet favor toward his own children, so our heavenly Father does the same. He goes ahead of us to open doors, lower mountains, raise valleys, and alert us to danger. He flies cover over us. He covers us from danger on our right flank, left flank, and rear flank. He delights in giving us good things and doing good things for us. And although He will allow us to face occasional persecution, trials, and setbacks in order to build faith within our hearts and character within our souls, He looks for every suitable opportunity to demonstrate His love and to prove to us that we are not just "anybody." We are His kids.

Before we move on, let me share with you this little recitation which I have used often in my life. I also use it with Christine to declare God's favor over our family and our home. Let me invite you to use it and even to memorize it so you can invoke it daily in your own life. When you learn to declare the favor of God, you will see the favor of God with more regularity in your life.

Lord, I thank You today for favor. I thank You that I am Your favorite child, which means I am particularly esteemed and have undue preference. I am the apple of Your eye. I am crowned with glory and honor, and because I wear a crown, that shows me that I am royalty. I have the character and status of a king. As part of the royal family, I can expect preferential treatment. Today, I declare favor in every area of my life: for my family, for my work, for the people I know and love, for my health and the health of those I care about, for my finances, in my travels, and in every little aspect of my daily life. Right now, I choose to recognize and accept the favor of God and to walk in all its benefits.

CHAPTER 2
OBEDIENCE

FAVOR IS GOD'S REWARD FOR OBEDIENCE

Now that we have taken an introductory look at favor and how it operates in your life through confession, let's take a closer look at the one precondition to favor: obedience. I believe that God rewards His people when they obey an instruction He gives them. God told Israel, "If you are willing and obedient, you will eat the best from the land" (Isaiah 1:19). The key word here is the little word *if*. The promises of God are always conditional; they are never *absolute*. In other words, the promises of God are offered to everyone, but only those who meet the preconditions of a particular promise will actually realize that promise in their lives. *If you are obedient*, you will eat the best of the land. Conversely, *if you are not obedient*, you won't necessarily eat the best of the land.

This cause-and-effect combination between our willingness to do something and God's willingness to bless us is evident throughout the Bible. For instance, the Bible tells us, "For God so loved the world, that he gave his only begotten Son, that whosoever believeth in him should not perish, but have everlasting life" (John 3:16, KJV). The Bible also tells us, "For the promise is unto you, and to your children, and to all that are afar off, even as many as the LORD our God shall call" (Acts 2:39, KJV). It says that the Lord is, "not willing that any should perish, but that all should come to repentance" (II Peter 3:9, KJV). So salvation and the subsequent gift of the Holy Spirit are free gifts that God offers to every man, woman, and child. God offers the gift of everlasting life because He loves those He has created and He doesn't want anyone to perish. But notice the connection that God repeatedly makes between an individual's willingness to do something and the activation of God's free gift of salvation in that person's life. Nobody is saved automatically. A person has to do something first in order to activate God's blessings in his life.

In the case of salvation, a person must believe in God's Son to be saved (John 3:16). Put another way, a person must intentionally "receive" Jesus as his or her Savior in order to be saved. As John noted earlier in his gospel, "As many as received him, to them gave he power to become the sons of God, even to them that believe on his name" (John 1:12, KJV). So salvation is activated through faith and by consciously receiving Christ as one's Savior. The promise of eternal life carries an accompanying prerequisite that must be fulfilled in order to activate the promise in one's life.

Sure, God loves the world so much that He gave His only begotten Son. But what good is that to me if I don't do something to respond to God's offer? The fact of the matter is that we do have to do something to activate God's promises in our lives. In the case of salvation, we have to believe and receive. In the case of forgiveness, we have to forgive those who have sinned against us if we want God to forgive us (see Matthew 6:14-15). In the case of prosperity, we have to open our own floodgates of blessing by showing generosity to those around us before we can hope to see God's bounty in our own lives (see Luke 6:38). And in the case of victorious living, we must learn to walk in the Spirit before we can see God's deliverance from the power of sin (see Galatians 5:16). Every biblical promise is activated by something we choose to do or it is made ineffective in our lives by something we choose not to do. So God's promises are free and available to all, but God's promises have preconditions that a person must meet in order to appropriate that particular promise for his life and in order to activate that particular promise in his life.

For every promise of God, there is an accompanying precondition that either activates that particular promise (through obedience) or nullifies it (through disobedience). This is why so many verses in the Bible begin with the little phrase, "If you..." or something similar. (Just check out Deuteronomy 28, for instance, particularly verses 1, 2, 9, and 13.) "If you will do certain things," God is saying, "then I will do something really awesome in response to your step of faith. I will enrich you by activating a reciprocal promise in your life." On the other hand, if you choose not to do something, there will be a reciprocal curse or lack of blessing (see Deuteronomy 28: 15, 58). So, obedience in some form is always attached to any promise that God makes, and though the promises may vary and the required acts of obedience may vary with them, the principle of obedience never varies. God blesses obedience, pure and simple.

So how does this pertain to the subject of favor? Simple! If you are planning to ask God to increase favor in your life, your lifestyle must first become a lifestyle of obedience. It must be pleasing to God. Your life must be set apart through obedience. This doesn't mean that you have to be perfect. Nobody is perfect, and the people God blessed in the Bible weren't perfect either. But they did obey God more often than not and they did obey Him in most of the areas of their lives. Because obedience was their lifestyle, they always picked themselves up whenever they stumbled and worked hard to learn how to walk in obedience in those areas of life that had caused them to stumble. God doesn't overlook sin and failure, but He does require obedience. Where there is obedience, there is blessing and favor. Where there is disobedience, there is chastisement and practical consequences that must be endured until obedience is learned.

I personally believe that the level of obedience in one's life determines the level of favor in his life. The two are intertwined, interrelated, interconnected, and reciprocal. Like peanut butter and jelly, like ham and cheese, they just go together. Like love and marriage, you can't have one without the other.

If you will read your Bible carefully and thoroughly, you will understand that obedience is the only thing God requires of us. He doesn't really want our money. He already owns all the money. He doesn't really need our talents. No matter how talented a man might be, there's somebody out there who can top what he does. He doesn't really care about our good deeds and good works, because to Him "all our righteous acts are like filthy rags" (Isaiah 64:6). He isn't impressed by our sacrifices, because, "I desired mercy, and not sacrifice; and the knowledge of God more than burnt offerings" (Hosea 6:6, KJV). In the economy of God's kingdom, obedience is the only currency that really counts. In fact, obedience is everything. It determines one's posture with the Lord. It determines one's status in the kingdom of heaven. It determines one's spiritual power and anointing right here on earth. It determines one's access to all of God's resources and promises. All God really wants from any of us is our obedience. He wants us to do what He says because acts of obedience prove our trust in Him, in His words, and in His motivations. And God is really impressed when we trust Him. In fact, faith and trust are the things He admires most and the qualities He most passionately responds to.

Consequently, if you want something from God (including His favor), you have to start obeying Him. If you want God involved in the important aspects of your life, you have to start demonstrating a lifestyle of obedience. I have been a Christian for a long time, and I have seen people pray for things and fast for things and work for things that they wanted from the hand of God. I have seen them step up their giving, step up their prayer life, and step up their participation in the church. Yet they still see no significant increase in God's involvement in the important aspects of their lives. Why? Because they have missed the point! It's not about giving more. It's not about praying more. It's not about going to church twice a week instead of once a week. There is no magic formula for making God do what you want Him to do. It's about obeying God. He wants our obedience in every area of our lives. That obedience can move His heart and move His hand on your behalf.

So if you want increased favor in your life, start obeying God in every area of your life. If you are a true believer, you probably already obey God in most of the areas of your life anyway. Besides, if you didn't obey God at least partially, people would know it and you would probably be too embarrassed to even go to church. At the same time, you know as well as I do that there are a few private areas in your life that you try to hide from God and others. You reserve those little rooms of your heart just for yourself. Oh, sure, you might let God have access to other areas of your heart and life, but you aren't about to let Him venture into these really private areas that you have convinced yourself you will deal with later. But those are the very areas that are hindering God's abundant favor in your life. You have tasted partial favor up until now because you have offered partial obedience. But now the Holy Spirit is calling you to a lifestyle of complete and open obedience. When you accept the divine call to that kind of lifestyle, you will begin to see a flood storm of favor in your life, because favor and obedience go hand in hand.

Allow me to illustrate the connection between obedience and favor by sharing with you an actual testimony from a farmer who lives in the Dallas area. I want to share this true story with you, because I think it powerfully illustrates the connection I am trying to make between man's obedience and God's favor. This farmer was a regular church attender. Richard (not his real name) was a faithful giver and a faithful man, and he knew the voice of God when God spoke to him. He was a good man, who always tried to do the right thing and always tried to obey the will of God as he understood it.

One day, when Richard was out in his fields plowing, the Holy Spirit spoke to him and said, "Go to the back corner of your property and drill for oil." But Richard hesitated. As so many of us do when we hear from God (and as many people did in the Bible), Richard procrastinated and rationalized. *There's no oil within 100 miles of here,* he thought, *so I must be imagining this.* Consequently, Richard continued plowing. But again, the Holy Spirit spoke to him and told him to go to the back corner of his property and drill for oil.

Richard did everything he could do to explain away the experience and to "reason" with that still, small voice he was hearing within his heart. But Richard was not a novice to the things of the Lord. He knew God's voice all too well, so he eventually decided to obey, and he dipped into his investments in order to hire the men and lease the equipment he needed to do the job. You probably already have guessed what happened. His friends and neighbors began to point and stare and talk. Everybody thought he was crazy, but Richard just pressed on. Like Noah, he knew that he had heard the voice of God. In fact, he was so sure that he had heard God's voice, he became quite willing to endure the laughter and ridicule of those around him. It was a necessary part of obeying God.

But people didn't laugh very long. It was just two days after he started drilling that Richard struck oil, and the newly dug well began to immediately produce about 600 barrels of oil each day. At that time, oil was selling at about $41 per barrel, so, if you figure it up, Richard was earning about $24,600 of extra backyard income every day, whether he was there or not, whether he was working or not. And he made this money simply by listening to God and obeying God's voice. How would you like to make almost $25,000 a day just for listening to God's voice and obeying a simple command from the Lord? Favor is God's reward for our obedience.

When Richard first heard God speak to him about drilling for oil, he had no idea that there was oil on his land. In fact, as I explained earlier, the nearest oil well was about 100 miles from Richard's farm, and no oil had ever been discovered on any land in that county or the next. But Richard had been walking on top of oil for a lot of years. Before Richard became the owner of his farm, others had walked on top of that same oil, never realizing that it was there. It was Richard's simple act of obedience that opened the floodgate of blessings for him, and now he is enjoying the best of the land. That is, he is enjoying the best houses, the best cars, the best clothes, and the best that life has to offer.

Richard now has ten oil wells that are producing an average of 2,000 barrels of oil per day. And since the current price of oil is hovering around $85 per barrel, that means he is raking in about $170,000 each and every day without doing anything to earn it. I would say that's a pretty good reward for walking in faith and a pretty good return on investment for simply obeying the voice of God.

Typically, God doesn't ask us to do strange or unusual things. I think He chose Richard for this blessing because Richard was a seasoned saint with a lot of personal experience when it came to hearing God's voice and obeying it. Richard had really "fine tuned" his spiritual ears, and he fully understood the difference between God's voice and his own internal self-talk. For the rest of us, however, obedience is simpler. God just wants us to do the right things in the right way every day. He wants us to listen to that tiny little voice deep inside our hearts that tells us "this is right" or "this is wrong." He wants us to heed those things that He challenges us to do when our pastors pour into us every Sunday morning, and He wants us to change our thinking and behavior just a little bit each day as we read His Word and try to apply it to our lives. The will of God does not consist of a few bizarre acts that make us look freakish; the will of God is a whole lot of little acts that make us look like we believe what we proclaim. Occasionally, God may ask us to do something that might seem a little illogical, but most of the time His will just makes good sense and our obedience is simply the right thing to do.

David declared, "The earth is the LORD's, and everything in it, the world, and all who live in it" (Psalm 24:1). This means that everything on top of the earth belongs to God and everything underneath the earth, as well. The cattle on a thousand hills belong to the Lord, and the hills belong to Him, as well. God has the resources, and quite often those resources are right beneath your feet, right beside you, or just slightly out of your reach. He can easily transfer possession of those resources from His hand to yours. But why would God want to bless somebody who doesn't have the Lord's best interests at heart? Why would He want to entrust you with more blessings when you have shown yourself incapable or unworthy of handling the blessings He has already placed at your disposal? It only makes sense that God would want to bless someone who has proven his faithfulness to God and to God's agenda. That kind of man can be trusted. That kind of woman is worthy of greater approval.

God is no fool. Even though many unrighteous people successfully acquire fortune and fame apart from God, they do so through much toil, great stress, and the constant fear of losing it or having it taken away. They must constantly fight and contend with others to keep what they have accumulated, and they must constantly use people and manipulate people to acquire what they have. Not so with the righteous! Not so with the favored people of God! Those men and women who are blessed because they obey God's voice and do the right thing are those who increase their wealth without struggle, who maintain their prosperity without fear, and who build a legacy of love and trust instead of hatred and scorn. They do not *earn* the best that life has to offer as much as they *receive* the best that life has to offer, and they receive it from the hand of God.

The Lord has made it clear that "every animal of the forest is mine, and the cattle on a thousand hills" (Psalm 50:10). In addition, "'The silver is mine and the gold is mine,' declares the LORD Almighty" (Haggai 2:8). So every living thing and every nonliving thing belongs to God. Whether man and animals, gold and oil, it all belongs to the Lord. He is quite willing to share what He has, because none of these things can really benefit Him personally. But they surely can improve the lives of those He loves. God's desire, therefore, is to share the riches of this world with those He loves. But He must see something within a person that "inspires" Him to pour out His bounty upon that individual, and the thing he looks for is faith expressed through obedience. "If ye love me, keep my commandments" (John 14:15, KJV).

Some people make the Christian life far too complicated and far too difficult, but the unvarnished truth is that the Christian life is really quite simple because God doesn't require a lot from us. He doesn't require us to be theologians. He doesn't require us to be professional clergymen. He doesn't require us to be weird or to withdraw from society. He just requires us to obey. In fact, obedience is the only thing God requires from us. It is your only responsibility before God. But what a potent thing it is, because not only does obedience stand as the only requirement for the child of God, it also serves as the entry point for all divine increase and all heavenly blessings.

Just start walking in obedience and see if the hand of God isn't magnified in your life and the blessings of God multiplied in your life. Just start doing those things that you already know to do because God has been telling you to do them for a long, long time. Start putting away those destructive behaviors that God has been telling you to lay down and start acting on the things you already know to be the will of God for your life. Then start looking for a noticeable increase in divine favor. Obedience and blessing, faith and favor! They fit perfectly together in God's economy, and one naturally follows the other. So become an obedient follower of Christ, and He will become your "rewarder of them that diligently seek him" (Hebrews 11:6, KJV).

BIBLICAL FACTS YOU SHOULD KNOW
ABOUT OBEDIENCE

- Obedience is doing anything God commands you to do, regardless of the cost.

- Your obedience guarantees that God will always respond in favor to you.

- Promotion always follows obedience.

- Your obedience to God's instruction is the only proof of your love for Him.

- Your obedience is rewarded with supernatural protection.

- Your obedience and faithfulness to your employer guarantees blessings from God.

- Your obedience to the Word of God creates increased favor in your life.

- Provision is only guaranteed at your point of obedience.

CHAPTER 3
SEEKING GOD

YOU CANNOT FIND WHAT YOU DO NOT SEEK

To find the queen is to find the source of the ants. To find the fire is to find the source of the smoke. To find God is to find the source of divine favor. But no man can find God, at least not in an intimate way, without first seeking Him. So the passionate pursuit of God himself is perhaps the very best pathway for increasing God's favor in your life. It's really quite simple: The more intimate you are with God, the more of His favor you will experience in your life. This is why the Bible encourages us to pursue God, to hunger for Him, and to seek His face.

Sure, in the beginning, while we are in a spiritually lost condition, God seeks us. He doesn't expect us to seek Him because we can't seek Him, so He becomes the seeker. Jesus said, "For the Son of man is come to seek and to save that which was lost" (Luke 19:10, KJV). In the beginning, Jesus is the Good Shepherd who leaves the 99 sheep in order to seek the one little lamb that is missing. He is the one who pursues and finds. Thank God that He is a seeking Savior. Otherwise, all of us would still be lost in sin.

But after a person is born again, God expects that person to turn the tables and to start seeking *Him*. He expects the presence of the Holy Spirit in an individual's life to compel that person to hunger and thirst for more of God's righteousness and to passionately pursue the person of God in order to satisfy his spiritual appetites. In fact, the Bible is replete with cries of spiritual hunger and with admonitions to seek the Lord. The psalmist declared, "As the deer pants for streams of water, so my soul pants for you, O God" (Psalm 42:1). The writer of Hebrews said, "He is a rewarder of them that diligently seek him" (Hebrews 11:6, KJV). And Jesus said, "Blessed are they which do hunger and thirst after righteousness: for they shall be filled" (Matthew 5:6, KJV). Spiritual satisfaction won't occur in your life until you learn to pursue God, finding Him in a more personal and intimate way.

Never forget that God created you in His own image. So if you want to understand the kind of relationship that God wants to have with you, there's a good chance that you can understand God's desire a little better just by taking a closer look at your own relational needs. You don't want a passionless life, and you don't want passionless relationships. You want some "fire" in your important relationships. You want some intimacy. You want openness and honesty and enthusiasm and zeal. So does God.

When I was younger, I wanted to get married. I hoped and prayed that, one day, I could find that perfect young lady I could love and who would love me in return. Of course, I wanted a good life with her, and I wanted to build a family with her and a ministry with her. But I also wanted to have intimacy in our relationship. I wanted some passion and some "sizzle." After all, those are the things that make marriage worthwhile and fulfilling. Who wants a "life sentence" with someone who is detached and boring? When I finally met Christine, however, that kind of relationship didn't just happen overnight. Sure, we were attracted to each other, and deep down inside, I think both of us knew that we were each other's gift from God. But Christine wanted to be pursued a little. She wanted me to show some excitement, some enthusiasm toward her. She wanted me to place her above everyone else in my life. What woman doesn't want that in a romantic relationship? Frankly, I wanted a little bit of that passionate pursuit myself. I wanted Christine to brighten up when I walked into the room. I wanted her to sound excited when I called on the phone. Man is designed to be wanted and pursued, and he is designed that way because he is designed in the likeness of God, who created him. God also wants to be loved, adored, and passionately pursued, and He is the rewarder of those who seek Him this way.

But how does God reward us for diligently seeking Him? How does He reward us for elevating Him to that status in our lives? He rewards us for seeking Him by providing us with more of His favor: "Now then, my sons, listen to me; blessed are those who keep my ways. Listen to my instruction and be wise; do not ignore it. Blessed is the man who listens to me, watching daily at my doors, waiting at my doorway. For whoever finds me finds life and receives favor from the LORD" (Proverbs 8:32-35).

In the Bible, there is a definite correlation between spiritual hunger and divine favor. Those in the Bible who truly sought the Lord were those who experienced His favor on a higher level. Just think about it! The great men who parted the waters, raised the dead, healed the sick, called down fire from the heavens, and foresaw the future were the same men who sought after God and hungered for

God. They were the same men who wrote the psalms and penned the instructions to us regarding spiritual hunger and thirst. But it was not the favor of God upon their lives that inspired them to seek God; it was their seeking hearts that inspired God to favor them. The spiritual hunger came first; the favor of God followed in the same way that a little puppy follows behind its master.

David is a great example of this. God favored David highly and exalted him above his seven brothers and all the other inhabitants of Israel. God made David king and gave him favor in battle, in leadership, and in spiritual legacy. But David was seeking the Lord long before he was anointed to be king, long before he killed Goliath, and long before God established an everlasting covenant with him. When he was young, David would take his harp and sing unto the Lord while he was tending his father's sheep. He would write love songs from his heart to the heart of God. All his life, David loved God and the things of God more than life itself. He danced in the presence of the Ark of the Covenant. He gave more offerings than perhaps any man before him. His greatest passion and purpose was to build a house for the Lord. David was a man of spiritual passion, and God favored David highly because of his seeking nature and his insatiable spiritual appetite, even naming His own begotten Son after this simple-hearted king.

In the New Testament, Peter, James, and John are great examples of this same principle. These three apostles experienced a higher level of favor than the rest of Jesus' disciples, but they experienced that increased favor because they refused to draw back from seeking a deeper relationship with the Lord or from going with Him into some of His most intense ministry situations. These three disciples were with Jesus when He was transfigured on the mountain. They were with Him when He raised Jairus' daughter from the dead. They were with Him when He prayed in the Garden of Gethsemane. These three men simply would not "settle" for the relationship they already had with Jesus. They wanted more of Jesus, and that spiritual desire inspired Jesus to draw them closer and favor them more highly.

Although God loves all His children equally, I believe that He favors them differently because of their varying capacities to appreciate and utilize His increased favor. To understand this distinction, just read your Bible. All of God's children will go to heaven, because heaven is a free gift of grace. But not all of God's children will be equal in heaven, because heavenly favor and eternal rewards are a result of spiritual achievement. Those who have given more will reap more. Those who have served more faithfully will be rewarded more abundantly. Those who humbled themselves on earth will be exalted in the everlasting kingdom. Salvation is free, but favor is earned. So those who are more serious about God are those who will derive more benefits from Him. Just as God, in the Old Testament, exalted David above all his brothers and just as Jesus, in the New Testament, exalted Peter, James, and John above their counterparts, so the Lord will exalt in heaven those who did more for Him on earth and will exalt on earth those who are dissatisfied with spiritual mediocrity in their present lives.

Jesus did not treat all people the same. He *loved* all people the same, but He did not *treat* them all the same. He loved them without precondition, but He treated them according to their individual character as manifested through their lives. He treated the twelve disciples differently than He treated the rest of His followers. He treated His followers differently than He treated the masses, who watched Him from afar and yet abandoned Him quickly. And He treated the masses differently than He treated the religious elite, who actually hated Him and opposed Him. He will treat you differently, too, if you can learn to touch the "tender spot" in His heart. If you can learn to desire Him, to want Him, to pursue Him, and to chase after Him until you find Him, you can join the ranks of David and Peter by moving to increased levels of favor in your life. When it comes to favor, God is prejudiced. He gives preferential treatment to those inside His inner circle. But unlike human beings, God does not restrict people from entering His inner circle. His invitation is open to all who will simply answer the call. So if you are willing to invest the necessary time and passion, you can go as deep into that "circle of trust" as you want to go, and you can receive as much divine favor as you can handle.

I have worked for various large ministries over the course of my life and I have found that the closer you are to the inner circle, the more favor you receive from the man of God. Unlike these inner circles of man, however, God's inner circle can accommodate a whole lot of people. While it takes a lot of time and talent to get a personal invitation to enter a human circle of trust, God's invitation to His circle is open to anyone who will accept it. Jesus said, "Go ye therefore into the highways, and as many as ye shall find, bid to the marriage" (Matthew 22:9, KJV).

There is one overriding thing that both these circles have in common: The closer you are to the person in the middle of the circle, the more likely you are to incur his favor. Promotion and prosperity await those inside God's circle of trust. The Lord himself has declared, "I love those who love me, and those who seek me find me. With me are riches and honor, enduring wealth and prosperity. My fruit is better than fine gold; what I yield surpasses choice silver. I walk in the way of righteousness, along the paths of justice, bestowing wealth on those who love me and making their treasuries full" (Proverbs 8:17-21). What favor! Riches and honor! Enduring wealth and prosperity! Gold and silver and treasuries that are full!

But precisely how does one go about seeking the Lord in such a way as to gain this kind of acceptance? Since you and I cannot ascend the Mount of Transfiguration with Peter, James, and John, and since we aren't harpists and songwriters like David, what exactly can we do to draw closer to God and to incur His increased favor in our lives? The only way I can possibly answer this question is to look at earthly love and romance, and then emulate that kind of love on a spiritual level with God. Remember, God created human beings in His own image, so if you can just take an honest look at the pure and sinless love needs of human beings, that's pretty much what God wants back from us. He created those desires within us, because He created us to be like Him.

With this in mind, I draw your attention to the five love languages defined by Gary Chapman. Chapman wrote a best-selling book entitled *The Five Love Languages* (Chicago: Northfield Publishing, 1992), in which he defined the five ways that human beings show love and receive love. Chapman's five love languages include words of affirmation, quality time, gift giving, acts of service, and physical touch. Let's take a brief look at each of these "languages" and then analyze how we can apply them to our pursuit of God.

Chapman reminds us that actions don't always speak louder than words. If words of affirmation is your love language, an unsolicited compliment may mean the world to you. If unsolicited words of affirmation can lift a human being to new heights of relational ecstasy, just think what similar words mean to God. In fact, if you think about it, that's all that worship really is. Worship is nothing more and nothing less than loving God with words of affirmation. By telling the Lord how much He means to us, how solidly we trust Him, and how much we desire Him, we touch His heart in a special way. When we thank Him, we touch His heart in a special way. And when we remind Him that there's nobody else above Him in our lives, we touch His heart in a special way. To draw nearer to God, learn to worship. Besides, worship is the only thing we do in this present world that will continue in the next world, so you might as well get in some practice.

How else do we show love to the important people in our lives? We show our love for them by spending quality time with them. By the way, "time" is not the same as "quality time." We can spend lots of time with people and never get to know them, because we are distracted by the television or by the chores that await us. But quality time involves our full, undivided attention. Nothing says "I love you," quite like this expression of worth. Setting aside the tyranny of the urgent to focus on that which is truly important, is one of the strongest and purest ways to express love. To avoid spending quality time with someone communicates loud and clear that they are not really that special and not really that loved. So spend time with God. How do you do that? Through the age-old methods of Bible study and prayer!

I believe that every Christian needs to spend time in God's Word, and I believe that it should be done on a daily basis. In fact, I believe that every Christian needs to spend time in God's Word the first thing every morning, because the way we start a day has a lot to do with the way we live that day. The Word of God is the believer's roadmap to successful living, and since each day is a journey, I think it's important to start each day's journey by checking the map for accurate directions. If you check the map at the end of the day, when the journey is over, you can't implement what you learn by reliving that particular day. You can only note where you went wrong so you can try to make course corrections on tomorrow's journey.

Many times, I have read my morning devotional, only to wonder what I was supposed to be getting from that portion of God's Word. Later in the day, however, I would encounter a particular situation that tied my daily Bible reading to real life, and it would all make perfect sense to me. If I had read the Bible later that night rather than in the morning, I would still be getting God's Word into my heart, but it would not have been applied to the situation I faced earlier that same day. God is sovereign, and quite frequently it seems that He orchestrates part of each day to align with the Scriptures we have been reading. I think He does this so the Word can be reinforced in our hearts as our brains tie it to our actual experiences and give it deeper personal meaning through the decisive events of our lives.

I also believe that every Christian needs to pray on a daily basis. Prayer is not complicated; prayer is simply talking to God. But in order to talk to God, you must take the time to talk to God. It doesn't happen while you sleep. Once again, I can use human relationships as a point of reference. If a person fails to spend time with the ones he loves, the love between them grows cold and intimacy becomes impossible. If I didn't spend time with my wife each day, for instance, she and I would grow apart and I doubt that our marriage would last very long. Relationships need to be nurtured, and nothing nurtures them quite like conversation during time together. That's all prayer is: conversation during time together. But just as I listen to Christine, as well as talk to her, so I need to listen to God, as well as talk to Him. In any relationship, if a person talks too much and listens too little while he is with the one he loves, he spoils the possibility for intimacy. The other person gets to know *him*, but he doesn't get

71

to know the other person's deepest thoughts and needs. So it is with prayer. In prayer, we listen as well as talk, because we want to get to know the God we follow and serve. If you are seeking answers from God regarding the important matters of your life, He can't give you those answers while you are talking. So learn to talk to God like you would talk with any close friend, and learn to listen so you can give Him opportunity to speak into your life.

The third love language, as defined by Chapman, is gift giving. Some people just love to receive gifts and their hearts are stirred whenever you think enough of them to take the necessary time and spend the necessary money to surprise them with an unexpected gift. For the receiver, it's not so much about the *thing* that they receive (people with this love language aren't materialistic), it's more about the thoughtfulness and the effort behind the gift. The one who receives a gift knows that he is important to the one who has given him the gift, and he knows that he is prized in the giver's heart above whatever was sacrificed to obtain that gift. To miss an important person's birthday, anniversary, or graduation would be a thoughtless gesture because it would deliver a message that the person is not very special. And so it is with God. God has made it clear in His Word that He loves gifts. In fact, He looks upon the giving of gifts as an act of worship. So you can touch the heart of God, create new levels of intimacy with Him, and incur His favor by showering Him with gifts in the form of offerings.

Closely associated with gift giving are acts of service. In his book, Chapman asks whether vacuuming the floors can really be an expression of love. Absolutely! By vacuuming the floors in your own home, you show your mate that you care. By vacuuming the floors in the house of the Lord, you show God that you care. By doing any act of service, you show that you place great worth upon the person you are serving and that you value that person's time and what he or she typically does for you. Service is a genuine expression of appreciation, so learn to express your love through discernible actions. In the kingdom of God, the highest position attainable is the position of servant. In fact, the first words that God will speak to His most favored followers on the day they enter His presence are the words, "Well done, thou good and faithful servant" (Matthew 25:21, KJV). So learn to show God how much you value Him and how highly you esteem Him by making yourself available to do some of those little things that can bless Him most. The Bible is full of suggestions. You can give a cup of cold water in Jesus' name. You can visit a widow or a prisoner. You can be kind to a child. You can help with the workload at God's house. Be creative, but be faithful. Reliable servants incur the favor of God.

The final love language noted by Gary Chapman is the language of physical touch. When it comes to marriage, this language isn't about the bedroom. It's about hugs, pats on the back, holding hands, and thoughtful touches on the arm, shoulder, or face—physical expressions that are meant to be reassuring and encouraging, not threatening or suggestive. Some people just simply respond to physical touch more than any other expression of love, and God delights in our "touch" too. Of course, because God is a spiritual being, we cannot hold His hand or pat Him on the back, but we can reach out to Him in the spirit and we can embrace His presence. We also can show our exuberance for Him through physical expressions of praise like clapping our hands, lifting our hands, shouting, or expressing our excitement about Him in other physical ways that are appropriate for the context in which we find ourselves.

The point is this: If we want God's unlimited favor, we must learn to draw closer to Him. To start the process of drawing closer, we must begin to seek a higher level of intimacy with Him. In the end, the favor you receive from God will be a direct consequence of the love you give to God, so start loving Him with at least as much passion as you show for the important people in your life and the important activities in your life, then let that love grow from there.

My desire for you is that you come to the place in your spiritual life where you can believe God for that which seems impossible. Remember that the only limitation you have in the area of faith and trust is your own lack of understanding of God's laws. But if you come to understand God's laws and His promises and you learn to activate them in your life, you can live in the land of promise every day. If you understand God's laws and His promises and you learn to activate them in your life, you can live in the land of increase every day. This is the land that the Bible speaks about when it describes "a land flowing with milk and honey" (Exodus 3:8, 17; 13:5; 33:3; Jeremiah 11:5; 32:22). This is the land of God's favor. But to dwell in this land of favor, you have to do the same thing that the Israelites did when they came to the land of promise. You have to get up and take it by faith. As King David proclaimed, "The lions may grow weak and hungry, but those who seek the LORD lack no good thing" (Psalm 34:10).

If you will begin to expect favor to flow into your life, then you can have favor in your life because we receive favor by faith, just as we receive anything else from God by faith. This principle is easy to demonstrate from Scripture, especially if you apply the age-old principle of first mention. You see, the first mention of any subject in the Bible is always significant and typically reveals a lot about how God feels regarding the matter at hand. With this in mind, the first mention of divine favor shows us the inseparable connection between favor and faith.

In Genesis 4, we read the story of Cain and Abel. The Bible tells us that "Abel kept flocks, and Cain worked the soil. In the course of time Cain brought some of the fruits of the soil as an offering to the LORD. But Abel brought fat portions from some of the firstborn of his flock. The LORD *looked with favor* on Abel and his offering, but on Cain and his offering he did *not look with favor*" (Genesis 4:2-5, emphases mine). So why did God "look with favor" upon Abel's offering while showing no favor for Cain's offering? The Bible explains this later in the book of Hebrews, when it declares, "By faith Abel offered God a better sacrifice than Cain did. By faith he was commended as a righteous man, when God spoke well of his offerings. And by faith he still speaks, even though he is dead" (Hebrews 11:4).

Faith, therefore, is the key that unlocks the favor of God in a person's life. Abel was the first man to receive favor from the Lord, and his receipt of that favor was prompted by faith and faith alone. By simply understanding that favor is still available today and by believing that God's promises of old can be God's promises for today, an obedient, God-seeking man (or woman) can accommodate all the favor of heaven for his present life on earth. But faith is the key. You see, every nation and every kingdom has its own currency. The United States has the dollar. Mexico has the peso. Japan has the yen. The United Kingdom has the sterling pound. The currency of the kingdom of God is faith. Faith is the only "commodity" that God recognizes when it comes to acquiring His blessings and appropriating His benefits for our lives.

According to the Bible, we can obtain from God anything we legitimately need as long as we have faith. We can have salvation. We can have healing. We can have financial blessing. And we can have increased favor. If God's people will simply believe what the Lord has promised to them through His Word, if they will only begin to see that God wants to apply His promises to their lives in this present world, and if they will seek Him more and more as they pursue Him with increasing passion, the Lord will be pleased to multiply His favor in their lives. So get excited about God—the person of God—and watch this Person of ineffable glory and splendor demonstrate His love for you in the same way you are demonstrating your love for Him: by finding your specific love language and doing everything imaginable to gratify all your needs in that area of your life. His favor awaits those who pour themselves out in pursuit of Him.

CHAPTER 4
EXCELLENCE

EXCELLENCE IS DOING THE BEST YOU
CAN WITH WHAT YOU HAVE

The dictionary defines excellence as "the quality of being outstanding or extremely good." It is the state of excelling at anything one seeks to do, the quality of being the very best of its kind. I also believe that excellence has a spiritual dimension. I believe it is the fulfillment of Jesus' directive to "go the extra mile" (see Matthew 5:41). It is the tendency of character to go above and beyond the call of duty, to do more than is expected of you, to give more than you receive, and to solve more problems than you create.

The Bible tells us in a couple of different ways that Jesus was a person of excellence. On the one hand, we learn from the gospel of Luke that "Jesus grew in wisdom and stature, and in favor with God and men" (Luke 2:52). Then we learn from the gospel of Mark that He did all things well (see Mark 7:37). Jesus was known for being above average. He was known for doing more than could rightly be expected of Him. He developed quite a reputation for being a man who did things with excellence. And, as a result, He grew in favor with both God and man.

Favor is undeniably linked to excellence. Just as we have seen a spiritual connection between favor and passion, between favor and obedience, and between favor and confession, so we must see the biblical and spiritual connection between personal excellence and divine favor. The reason so few people have God's favor upon their lives is because they fail to see these connections and they fail to pay the price to attract God's favor and to retain it. All these factors are linked. Basically, to grow in the grace of God and to grow closer to God is to grow in favor with both God and man. But few people will ever pay the high price for this kind of favor, because even though God's favor is free, it isn't cheap. To have favor on your life, you must seek the Lord, say the same things about yourself that He is saying, believe Him, trust Him, and obey Him in all things. You also must rise above the human tendency for mediocrity and stand head and shoulders above all those around you when it comes to the important aspects of your life. You must demonstrate excellence.

When Jesus commissioned His followers to "go the extra mile," He was basically telling them to do more and to go farther than mere men could ever hope to go. When the average person is slapped on the cheek, for instance, he won't respond by offering his other cheek. When the average person has his tunic stolen, he won't offer the thief his cloak, as well. When the common man loans money that becomes uncollectable, he won't respond by forgiving the debt. And the individual who is compelled against his will to walk a mile certainly won't offer to walk two. But in the Sermon on the Mount, this is the very call to excellence that Jesus put forth to those who would take up His mantle (see Matthew 5:38-48). Jesus wanted those who bear His name to rise above the fray, to stand head and shoulders above their contemporaries, and to demonstrate His presence in their lives, not with their words alone, but also with their deeds. Deeds that would go above and beyond the call of duty! Deeds that would be "outstanding or extremely good"! Deeds of excellence!

What Jesus was saying is that there's a lot of traffic on the first mile of any journey. A lot of people—even unbelieving people—are willing to go one mile. But the moment you get to that second mile (or any additional miles), there's hardly anyone on the highway. And that's the point. If God's people are *supposed* to be different, then we *should* be different. We shouldn't blend in. We shouldn't be beige. We shouldn't be "average." We should excel. We should think differently, speak differently, and act differently than those who have no hope. We should live what we preach. We should practice what we believe and live out what we claim to hold dear. We should excel.

Jesus continued to hammer this theme of excellence throughout His earthly ministry when He asked, "For if ye love them which love you, what reward have ye? do not even the publicans the same? And if ye salute your brethren only, what do ye more than others? do not even the publicans so?" (Matthew 5:46-47, KJV). In other words, be excellent. Do more than is expected of you. Shock people. Mesmerize people. Live by a higher standard. Pay more attention to the quality of your own behavior than you do to the quality of other people's behavior. Think of yourself as spiritual royalty and conduct yourself accordingly. After all, you are the child of a King and you do bear a family resemblance to your heavenly Father. You also are a friend of God, so you are special. And excellence—not self-righteousness or spiritual pride—is the quality that sets you apart. Consequently, you should do what others refuse to do. You should go where others refuse to go. You are rare indeed, so you should leave an imprint on every person you encounter. As a result, the favor of man will follow you and the favor of God will seek you out.

Are you beginning to see that God doesn't want His kids to do just enough to get by in life? They bear His name and represent Him to a watching world, so God wants His kids to excel. He wants them to be the very best at whatever they choose to do so God can receive the glory that shines through their lives. In God's way of thinking, "just good enough" isn't good enough. In God's economy, excellence is the only acceptable standard, and excellence is simply doing your best with what God has given to you.

Christians, therefore, should be the best businessmen. They should be the best teachers. They should be the best musicians, the best cooks, and the best soldiers. They should be model citizens. They should be model students. They should drive the cleanest cars. They should have the best-kept lawns. They should wear the cleanest and most appropriate clothes. They should do the kind of work that never requires a follow-up effort. They also should exhibit the best attitudes while they do these things.

One thing I definitely believe is that Christians should be the best workers, because our work consumes a huge portion of our waking lives. Christians who are bosses, therefore, should be the best bosses. They should honor their employees, treat them with respect, reward them for faithfulness, and pay them generously. At the same time, those who are not bosses should be model employees. They should work hard, be honest in all their dealings with the company, speak honorably of their employers, and represent their companies well in the marketplace. A believer who cuts corners on the job or joins other employees in bad-mouthing the company is not worthy of God's favor.

The Bible has a lot to say about the way bosses should treat their workers and the way workers should treat their bosses. The Bible basically encourages those in a position of authority to respect those who serve them and to honor those who are financially dependent upon them. Bible writers, from Moses to Paul, command bosses to pay fair wages and to treat their workers with dignity. At the same time, the Bible repeatedly commands workers to give the very best of their time and talents to their bosses and to look out for the well being of their employers.

As Christians, therefore, we should be the hardest working people on any job site. We should never be the ones standing by the time clock at 4:59, waiting to punch out so we can run to our cars, especially if we refused to run to our various assigned tasks during the workday. Instead, we should be the first ones to clock in and the last ones to clock out, the first ones to be available for overtime and the last ones to call in sick. We should give more than we take, and we should do more than is required of us.

Statistics prove that people in the United States are among the hardest-working people in the world. We work longer days than most of the rest of the world. We work longer weeks. We take less vacation time, and we retire later in life. This is part of the reason we are among the most productive nations in the world. Nevertheless, this doesn't make me feel great about my own country as much as it makes me feel bad about the rest of the world, because I just don't see that much work ethic in the United States. My experience tells me that most people do just enough to get by, and little more. Employees seem more interested in their benefits than their productivity; more concerned with their breaks than their customers. If you drive down the street of any community in America, you can see workers huddled outside the back entrance to their stores, smoking and talking. You can see idle utility workers standing around open potholes or piles of sand. You can see slow moving truck drivers barely making their way toward their next work assignment. I am convinced that if we abolished the hourly wage in this country and started paying people strictly on the basis of what they produced, many of them would starve. But those with attitudes of excellence would thrive, because favor, as well as prosperity, follows those who give their all.

If you want to walk in the favor of God, then you have to give an honest day's work for an honest day's pay. And if you don't think the pay is honest, then give an honest day's work anyway (your "extra mile") while you look for a better job. If you truly have qualities of excellence, you won't have much trouble finding a better job. Wherever you work, you should be the one setting an example for others with your work ethic and your attitude. That is what God demands of you if you desire His favor and His blessings.

A strong work ethic is one of the most important things a winner can possess. In fact, men and women of excellence never see work as a negative thing. They realize that work is a "God-thing," a blessing which God designed for man in Genesis 2, long before sin entered the picture and long before God cursed the world. Some people mistakenly believe that work is a curse, that it was God's punishment on Adam for eating the fruit of the tree, but that's just not true. God's curse on Adam was a curse of hard labor and little return. God told Adam that, as a consequence for his sin, he would now eat his bread "by the sweat of your brow" (Genesis 3:19). In other words, Adam and his descendants would now have to labor harder in order to produce less. They would have to fight thorns and thistles and the cruelty of the elements in order to extract their living from the ground, and their excessive efforts would create a lot of sweat and a lot of pain.

God's curse made it harder to get the desired results from our work, but work itself was never a curse. In fact, it was one of the seven blessings God gave to man when the world was perfect and sinless in order to make man's life enjoyable and meaningful. God planted a garden, placed the man He had created in the garden, and gave him the responsibility for tending the garden and keeping it. In other words, God gave Adam a job. Oh, and by the way, He gave him a job before He gave him a wife, but I'll save that teaching for another chapter and another day.

The point is that work is a blessing, not a curse. It is the mechanism through which a man finds his purpose, fulfills his calling, and leaves his legacy for future generations. To approach one's livelihood with contempt or mediocrity, therefore, is to despise God's gift. So get with it! If you just cannot force yourself to see your current job as a channel for God's blessings in your life, then get a new job, but find the place that God has for you and treat every professional milestone along life's journey as if it is God's assigned post for you at that moment. On your job, treat people wonderfully. On your job, do excellent work that speaks highly of you and the God you serve. On your job, leave a legacy and a sweet smelling savor unto the Lord.

Margaret Thatcher said, "I do not know anyone who has gotten to the top without hard work." So work hard. This is glorifying to God. Be sure to seek every opportunity to go that extra mile for the sake of your testimony and for the sake of the Lord's name. When you bear the name of the Lord and you reflect His character in the workplace, you might have to stay later to get an important project finished or to honor a commitment you made to your boss.

You might have to skip lunch in order to make sure things are in order for the monthly review. You might have to entertain important clients on your day off. You might even have to work through a salary cutback if sales in your particular industry have declined. But if you show the character of Christ on your job, you will do whatever is necessary… and then some… to exhibit excellence in your work. After all, you are a child of God, and the Lord has called you to do more with what He has given to you.

If you live "the extra mile" mentality and if you practice "the extra mile" in the workplace, I cannot promise you that life will always be easy, but I can promise you three things. First, when your life has concluded here on this earth, you will be greatly rewarded in heaven. Second, when people remember you and speak of you, they will describe your life as an example of Christian character. You will definitely impact those who watch you over the years. And third, you will enjoy increased favor in your life as long as you live in this world. You will enjoy the favor of your family. You will enjoy the favor of your friends. You will enjoy the favor of your employer and those who worked alongside you on a daily basis. You will also enjoy higher income and the favor of God.

If you have been a Christian long enough to learn some things about God's nature, you know that God is self-sacrificing. He is a giver, because it is His nature to give. You also know that God commands His people to be givers too, and that He favors those who answer His call to give. God blesses financial givers by giving back to them "good measure, pressed down, shaken together and running over" (Luke 6:38). Excellence is a form of giving too, because excellence is simply giving more than is expected of you. Just as God rewards those who give financially, He also rewards those who "go the extra mile" on His behalf. How does God "give back" to those who show excellence in their lives? How does He show them His favor in this world? The same way He blesses financial givers—by prospering them through the hands of others! Remember, Jesus said that God would bless financial givers by causing men to pour into their laps. If you do excellent work, therefore, you should expect to reap financial favor from God in the same way - through the hands of others, particularly your employer.

Lee Iacocca, the former chairman of the Chrysler Corporation, said, "The kind of people I look for to fill top management spots are the eager beavers, the mavericks. These are the guys who try to do more than they're expected to do." People of greatness are not impressed with "average." People of greatness are impressed with excellence. God, who is truly great, also is impressed with greatness. But unlike corporate executives, God doesn't look for greatness in the one or two big "performances" of our lives. He looks for excellence in all that we do, especially the little things, the small things, the routine things of life. He looks for excellence in our work, in our efforts as parents, in our volunteer work at church, in the casual conversations we have with ordinary people in everyday life.

Mike Murdock, the renowned pastor and evangelist and one of my mentors in ministry, said, "The key to your future is hidden in your daily routine." I agree with him. You have to start your day, every day, in full gear, not neutral, because real life is lived in the ordinary moments of every day and those moments begin when you get up in the morning.

As I have explained, God's desire for His children is that we do the very best we can with the talents and resources He has placed at our disposal. But this definition of excellence carries two important thoughts with it. First, if you are doing the best you can do with the talents and resources God has given to you, then you cannot perform at a level that is beneath your own capabilities and still be "excellent." I have commented at length about this reality and explained it fully. The second thought is just as important. If you intend to do the best you can do with the talents and resources God has given to you, you cannot expect to perform at a level above your capabilities either. Each man and each woman has a God-given potential, and that is all that God expects from us.

When Jesus shared with His disciples the parable of the three servants, He described a master who was preparing to take a long journey. Before leaving, this master entrusted ten talents, five talents, and one talent respectively to each of his three servants. According to the parable, the master gave responsibilities to the servants "each according to his ability" (Matthew 25:15). He did not entrust ten talents to the man who was only capable of handling one talent, and he did not entrust to the most talented servant the responsibility of managing only a single talent. Jesus knows your capacity for service, and He knows mine. He will not give you more than you can bear, but He also will not give you less.

When the master returned from his journey, he called each of his three servants to appear before him to give an accounting for the specific responsibility entrusted to him. When the master learned that the first servant had converted his ten talents into twenty talents, he rewarded (favored and blessed) that servant for his excellence in service. When the master learned that the second servant had converted his five talents into ten talents, he also rewarded (favored and blessed) that servant for his excellence in service. But when the master learned that the third servant had done nothing with the single talent entrusted to his care, the master had that servant removed from his household and severely punished.

We learn two things from this parable regarding excellence. First, we learn that the Lord expects *something* from each of us. He won't accept mediocrity and He won't accept "average." When it comes to His heavenly rewards and His earthly favor, He won't bless people who hide their talents and do nothing with them.

Second, we learn that the Lord rewards His servants equally for unequal returns. He gave the same reward to the servant who earned ten talents and the servant who earned five. Why? Because both of these servants were faithful with the number of talents entrusted to them by their master. The master didn't expect the servant with less resources to do as much as the servant with more resources. Both of them showed excellence by handling their respective talents well, so both of them received equal praise, even though one of them had more talents to begin with.

God gives things to people in different measures. In the New Testament, we are told that He gives each man a "measure of faith" (see Romans 12:3). He gives individuals their own unique measure of blessing (see Romans 15:29), their own unique measure of the fullness of Christ (see Ephesians 4:13), and He gives individual believers their own unique manifestation of the Spirit (see I Corinthians 12:7). God doesn't treat His children alike any more than an earthly father treats his children alike. He can't. Each of His children is unique and each one is different. But like an earthly father, God does treat each of His children according to that child's unique capabilities, helping that child to nurture his specific strengths while overcoming his specific challenges.

So if you have a gift for singing, learn to sing better than anybody else. If you have a special talent for cooking, be the best cook you can be and enrich the lives of others through your culinary craft. If you have a special ability to talk with hurting people and to listen to them with empathy, then regard that talent as God's gift to you and to others through you. If you can drive nails and saw lumber with the best of them, then hone those skills and ask God to show you ways to use them to benefit His kingdom. Do the very best you can do with what God has given you.

Being excellent means that you learn to focus on the one or two things God has given you to do with a level of skill that other people seem unable to equal. At the same time, being excellent means doing everything else in your life to the best of your limited abilities. You should always be honored to serve God and bless others through the things you do best, but you should never be ashamed of the things you cannot do at a level with others. You should know your own capabilities, and you should know your own limitations. This means you should never, ever fall victim to the tendency to think lowly of yourself by focusing on those things that you don't do as well as others. Why? Because comparing yourself to someone else is one of the stupidest things you can do! On the day of reckoning, God won't give His assessment of you by holding you next to someone else's standard; God will judge you by holding you up against your own potential. Where you had great talents, He will require more of you, and where you had fewer talents, He will not expect as much. But He *will* require excellence across the board (the best you could do with what you had). Perhaps Jesus put it best when He said, "From everyone who has been given much, much will be demanded; and from the one who has been entrusted with much, much more will be asked" (Luke 12:48).

God knows what you have the capacity to do, and He will hold you accountable to do that. Nothing more, and nothing less! Excellence is the Creator's rightful demand. Just as He expects an apple tree to be a good apple tree and to yield apples for Him, not oranges, and just as He expects sparrows to produce more sparrows, not eagles, so He expects you to develop the talents and skills He has placed within you, not the talents and skills He has placed within someone else. Yet He expects you to do everything you do with the highest level of excellence you can muster for that particular task. God looks with favor upon that which gives Him His rightful return on investment. He doesn't expect more, and He won't settle for less.

Be aware, therefore, that we cannot expect God to increase us in favor or in any other area of life if we are not willing to do our best. It's that simple. God made everything in creation to give Him a return on His investment. He made you to give Him a return on His investment. God won't be pleased with you, therefore, and He certainly won't reward you if you are not doing what you were created to do, nothing more and nothing less.

So demonstrate through your life that you are ready for more of God's favor. Prove yourself faithful with what you have, and God will give you more responsibility and more corresponding blessing. You cannot expect God to give you a new car if you can't keep your current car clean, so try vacuuming the French fries from between the seats of your old car before you start praying for a new car. Likewise, you can't expect God to give you a new house if you don't take care of the one you have right now. So before you start asking God for a bigger house in a nicer neighborhood, try mowing the lawn at the house you live in today and try setting an example for the rest of your neighbors by maintaining your lawn to its highest capacity. But the list goes on! You can't expect God to give you new clothes if you never iron the clothes you wear right now. You can't expect God to give you a new job if you're not excelling at the one you have right now. Do you get the point?

People pray all the time for newer, bigger, better, and brighter things from God, but they have never demonstrated their appreciation and respect for the things that God has given them in the past, so why would God want to give them more? I have learned that God will give you all that you can handle, but He will never give you more than you can bear. So if you can't clean the small house you own right now, why would God want to burden you with a bigger house in the future? If you find it too difficult to wash your old car today, why would God want to burden you with a bigger car tomorrow? Show God your faithfulness with that which He has already entrusted to you, and He will be inclined to entrust you with more.

Joel Osteen, senior pastor at Lakewood Church in Houston, has been perhaps the greatest example of excellence I have seen in my life and ministry. I have learned so much by watching this wonderful man of God and good friend in a lot of different situations, and I count it an honor to emulate him in his ceaseless pursuit of excellence. I have actually seen Pastor Joel point out out a single, small light that was out up in the tresses. Then I have watched his excellent staff repair that light by the end of the workday. Whether I observe his work, his house, his car, or the clothes he wears, I always see excellence in Joel Osteen's life. He exudes excellence, and he models it for others. I have never seen Pastor Joel do less than his very best for God, and I have told pastors and parishioners across this country that they need to visit him and learn from him. He is indeed a model of excellence.

The Bible tells us that Jesus was the greatest model of excellence. According to one of the eyewitnesses of His life and ministry, Jesus did "all things well" (Mark 7:37, KJV). This fact is recorded for us, not only so we might look up to Christ as we come to appreciate who He is, but also to stir us and inspire us to follow in His footsteps through the power of the Holy Spirit. If Jesus did all things well, it is because He wants us to do all things well, too. In fact, through Solomon, God told us as much when He said, "Whatever your hand finds to do, do it with all your might" (Ecclesiastes 9:10).

Excellence is God's way. Excellence is the Jesus-style of life and ministry (work). Excellence is what God expects from us as a return on the investment He has made in us over the course of our lives. Excellence, also, is the foundation of all God's blessings, because He blesses and favors those who do His bidding and fulfill His purposes in the earth to the best of their abilities. Become a channel of excellence in all that God has given you to do and you will certainly see His hand upon you and His favor around you. You will surely see Him lift you above your fellows as He demonstrates His preference for you in the sight of an onlooking world. His favor will always follow your excellence.

CHAPTER 5
PROBLEM SOLVING

SOLVING A PROBLEM FOR SOMEONE ELSE IS ONE OF
THE SUREST WAYS TO OBTAIN GOD'S FAVOR

In this book, I have already mentioned Dr. Mike Murdock. I have quoted him in the text, and I have referred to him as a source of inspiration and motivation. Obviously, Dr. Murdock has played an important role in my life. Not only has he poured rich wisdom and insight into my life, he also has taken me under his wing to teach me the things of the Lord and to mentor me in the work of the ministry. Have you ever stopped to contemplate the ways that the important people in your life actually came into your life? Quite often, the important people in my life came into my life because of a common problem that brought us together, perhaps at work, perhaps at school, or perhaps in life or in service to God.

I recall fondly the first time that I met Mike Murdock. I was young and relatively new to the ministry, and I was on a ministry-related trip to Dallas with another minister. While I was in the Dallas-Fort Worth, area, I took some time to visit a friend of mine who lived nearby and who worked for Dr. Murdock at the time. In fact, I visited my friend at his office.

While visiting my friend at the offices of what is now The Wisdom Center, I was introduced to Mike Murdock personally. Unfortunately, my friend introduced me to Dr. Murdock while he was in the middle of an intense discussion with two of his employees. Obviously, because I had walked into the middle of that discussion, I was not privileged to all that had been said before my arrival. Nevertheless, it was obvious to me that these men and women were trying to solve a problem. Dr. Murdock needed to be in Florida on a particular date, and he was trying to arrange an itinerary that would allow him to travel there on his preferred date and keep him busy until he returned home on another preferred date.

Without being asked, I decided that I was going to take a stab at trying to solve this perceived problem. I don't exactly know why I wanted to jump into the middle of this problem. I guess it's just natural for God's people to want to help others, especially those who have helped them through their service to God. So I went into my friend's office, picked up the phone, and called another friend of mine, Dr. Dan White, who was a true "father" in the Lord to me. Dr. White was the senior pastor of Jacksonville Christian Center in the same city where Dr. Murdock needed to be. I asked Dr. White if he would be willing to schedule Mike Murdock for pulpit ministry on that particular Sunday. He took a quick look at his church calendar and said that he would be happy to have Dr. Murdock on that day. He noted the date on his calendar, and we concluded our conversation.

As soon as I got off the phone, I went back to the room where Dr. Murdock and his team were discussing possible solutions to their problem, and I told them that I had just communicated with a pastor in Jacksonville who would love to have Dr. Murdock speak in his church on the date the team needed to fill. Needless to say, everyone was happy, especially Mike Murdock. That moment became a pivotal moment in my life. Without really contemplating the ramifications of my actions, I had solved a problem for a man who had a lot of friends and a lot of influence. He was truly in a position to bless my life, and he did. In fact, that initial encounter with Mike Murdock has brought great favor into my life and has been directly responsible for the direction of my life since then.

While I was there in Texas, I got to know Dr. Murdock a little better and when the time came for me to return home, Dr. Murdock asked me if I would be willing to stay behind so I could take a trip with him to Ohio. Since my work with this other minister was finished, I accepted Dr. Murdock's invitation and traveled with him to Ohio. In fact, I traveled with him everywhere he went for the next three months. Needless to say, we became very close, and I was invited into his inner circle of confidentiality and trust. It was there that my current ministry developed and from that platform that it was launched.

What occurred to bring me such opportunity? What happened that moved me from the fringes of obscurity and from the mere role of a friend of an employee to the level of a trusted associate and ministry partner in a single day? What was it that brought such divine favor into my life? Simple! I solved a problem for the man, and that one tiny act of problem solving produced more favor in my life and ministry than any other act I have ever performed. My willingness to solve a problem for Dr. Murdock must have made a lasting impression on him, because, for the next three years, I took care of all of his scheduling. In addition, Christine and I had the opportunity to travel around the world with Dr. Murdock, learning the ins and outs of ministry from one of the greatest evangelists of our time. If that is not favor, I don't know what is. But all of these good things happened to me for a reason. All these fantastic opportunities were created by something I did. I solved a problem for someone else, and that one act opened the floodgates of blessing in my life.

I want you to begin to look for problems you can solve. In fact, if the Spirit of God lives within you, the whole thrust of your life should be about solving problems for others. Jesus solved problems every day. He forgave sins that were weighing people down. He imparted wisdom that changed people's lives. He straightened withered limbs. He opened blinded eyes. He fed hungry people. Jesus was all about solving problems, and your life should be driven by the same motivation.

Not every problem you solve will open a door of opportunity for you right away, but that shouldn't matter. You should just live your life to solve problems for those around you, for the people you love and even for people you just met. Your spouse has problems that you can help solve (believe me when I tell you that this will truly enhance your marriage). Your boss has problems that you can help solve (and this will give you job security like nothing else can). Your pastor has problems that you can help solve. In fact, everybody you know has a problem that you can help solve. If you will just begin to solve problems for the people in your sphere of influence, that one change in purpose will do more to increase favor in your life than anything else you can do. Just find the problem that you are the answer to and then solve that problem for someone else.

In case I have opened up a whole new paradigm of life for you, let me share with you a few things the Bible teaches about problems and about solutions to problems. If you can fully grasp these biblical truths, they could change your life forever.

LIFE ITSELF IS PROBLEMATIC

I know this is a harsh thing to say, but it is true. Yes, Jesus made a lot of promises to those who believe and every one of those promises will come true, but while some of God's promises to us focus on this world, a lot more of them focus on the world to come. This means that we have to deal with a lot of unpleasant stuff in this world while we wait for the fulfillment of God's promises in the world to come. And that isn't easy. In the meantime, life is filled with problems.

Jesus said, "In the world ye shall have tribulation" (John 16:33, KJV). I know this is not the kind of divine promise that we want to mount in a frame or print on a bumper sticker. Nevertheless, these words of Jesus are just as real and just as true as His promise to never leave us or forsake us. Jesus will never leave us or forsake us because we need Him. While we are still in this world, there will be a lot of problems that are hard to deal with. Life is problematic.

I am known, by many, as a life coach and an inspirational speaker, but I didn't choose my line of work by accident. I became a Christian life coach because I am a very positive and optimistic person. I don't have to manufacture hope or excitement; I radiate hope and excitement. Nevertheless, I have a realistic view of life and I know that life is problematic. Life in this world can be cruel, unkind, unjust, and unfair. I believe that the promises of God are true, but I also believe that a lot of problems lie between God's promises and God's provisions. Even though I try to get people to focus on the provisions of God that lie on the other side of their problems, I still want people to have their own realistic view of life. Nothing defeats Christians quite like unrealistic expectations, so I don't want to be guilty of encouraging those unrealistic expectations. When a believer has false expectations of life, he sets himself up for failure no matter how optimistic he might try to be, because disappointment and discouragement are the offspring of unrealistic expectations.

As a starting point from which to work, therefore, always view life the way that it really is, not the way that it should be in a perfect world. Then look at the promises of God for the specific challenges you face and ask yourself what you need to do to activate those promises in your life. This two-step process can move you from "here" to "there." It can help you travel from the problem to the solution. But if you aren't willing to face the fact that life has problems, you are going to become bitter at God and discouraged with life. You are going to become disenchanted too, and your enthusiasm for life will wane.

I'm not trying to be negative here. I actually believe that for every problem, God has a solution and you are often part of God's solution to a problem (that is the point of this chapter). But the reason God has solutions is because problems exist. We Christians need to face this reality of life. It is the nature of life in a fallen world to be riddled with continual problems.

BETWEEN THE PROMISE AND THE PROVISION, THERE IS ALWAYS A PROBLEM

Every time God made a promise to someone in the Bible, there was substantial "lag time" between the day God made that promise and the day He fulfilled it. In addition, problems always arose during that "lag time" to make the wait more difficult. God made a promise to give Abraham a son, but it was about 25 years before that promise was fulfilled. God gave Joseph a dream when he was a very young man, but at least a dozen years passed before that prophetic dream became a reality. God promised the patriarchs a land that their descendants could call their own, yet it was nearly 700 years after the initial promise was made before the Jews actually took possession of the Promised Land. God promised King David that one of his descendants would sit on his throne forever, but it took approximately 1,000 years before the Messiah was born.

The promises of God in the Bible were rarely fulfilled overnight. Most of them took time. Just as a newly conceived baby needs to grow in the womb before it can be born as a healthy boy or girl, so God needs time to align people, circumstances, and other factors before He can bring His promises to fruition. There is a "gestation" period for the promises of God, where God is working invisibly behind the scenes to line up all the elements of His promise in order to ultimately manifest the promise He has made. Eventually, "in the fullness of time," God will make good on His promises (see Galatians 4:4). But these things take time. Besides, when you're God, what's the hurry?

But this delay always presents problems for us. Between the promise of God and the provision of God, there are always problems to solve. Abraham's problem during his 25-year wait for Isaac was the problem of sustaining his faith in the face of the passing years and remaining faithful to the Lord during that long period of childlessness. Joseph's problem during his long wait for his brothers to bow down to him was the problem of enduring suffering and remaining faithful to God during many difficult years of slavery and imprisonment. The problem of the patriarchs during their 700-year wait to occupy the Promised Land was the problem of four centuries of slavery and the problem of successfully traversing the wilderness under the leadership of Moses. And the problem of King David and the rest of the nation of Israel during their 1,000-year wait for the Messiah was the problem of consistently serving the Lord and dealing with the enemies that would destroy them in the meantime.

Every promise of God has its ultimate provision. God will always provide what He has promised, but between the promise and the provision, there will always be problems. God has designed it that way. Only in the face of problems can we grow. Only in the face of problems can we learn to trust God. Only by overcoming our problems can we truly appreciate God's provision on the other side of the problems. Only by enduring the problems of life can we learn perseverance, patience, and the other commendable qualities of life.

THERE ARE SOME PROBLEMS
THAT ONLY GOD CAN SOLVE

God certainly wants to use you and me to make a difference in people's lives, but there are a whole lot of things we cannot do. In the end, we have to trust God to do things that we humans cannot do. We cannot save lost souls. We cannot force people to make right decisions. We cannot heal the sick or open the spiritual eyes of those who cannot see God at work in their lives. There are a lot of things we *can* do for God and for others in this life, but one of the keys to spiritual maturity and effectiveness is knowing the difference between those things God has given us to do on His behalf and those things we cannot do at all.

Some people try to play God. They have a Messianic complex. They believe it is up to them to right all the world's wrongs and to solve all the world's problems, but many things are beyond the scope of human ingenuity. At some point, the effective servant of God must come to realize that there are things he cannot do. One of the most famous prayers that has ever been prayed is the Serenity Prayer of Reinhold Niebuhr, who prayed, "Lord, grant me the serenity to accept the things I cannot change, courage to change the things I can, and wisdom to know the difference." You and I need to know the difference between those things God expects us to do for others in His name and those things that we cannot do at all. We should passionately engage the things we can change, and we should relinquish with faith those things we cannot change. In faith, we should leave the work of God to God himself.

YOU AND I WERE CREATED TO
SOLVE MANY OF LIFE'S PROBLEMS

What other meaningful purpose do we have? In fact, in the Bible it is amazing how often God used people to solve problems that He could have solved with the blink of an eye. Look at the miracles of Jesus, for instance. When Jesus fed the 5,000, He was the one who worked the miracle (the part of the problem-solving process that human beings could not do), but He waited until a young boy stepped forward with two fish and five loaves of bread before He acted. Once the boy did the part that he had the capacity to do, Jesus did the part that the boy did not have the capacity to do. Jesus did the miraculous part.

Notice that Jesus also involved His disciples in the feeding of the 5,000. Before Jesus did the miraculous part, He commanded His disciples to do those things that they were capable of doing. Jesus commanded His disciples to seat the people in organized groups. Jesus commanded His disciples to bring the fish and bread to Him. Jesus commanded the disciples to distribute the fish and bread to the masses. Jesus commanded His disciples to take up the leftover pieces and place them in baskets. Jesus did not do anything to affect a miracle until His disciples did everything they could do first to obey His commands and to serve the needs of the people. Jesus didn't even get involved until His servants had done everything possible on a natural level to solve the problem at hand.

This pattern is visible everywhere in the ministry of Jesus Christ. His very first miracle, in Cana of Galilee, was similar. Somebody came to Jesus with a problem: There was no more wine. But Jesus did not lift a finger to solve the problem on the miraculous level until the servants first did everything they could do to solve the problem on a natural level. Eventually, Jesus changed the water into wine, and that is a miracle that no man could manufacture, but before Jesus worked this miracle, He commanded the servants of the house to bring Him the empty jars. Then He commanded the servants to fill the jars with water. Then He commanded the servants to dip the water out of the jars. Then He commanded them to serve the contents of the jars to the guests. Only after the servants had done all that they could do, was Jesus willing to do the part that they could not do. Miracles follow faithful service.

I can see this approach to problem solving duplicated in almost every one of Jesus' miracles. He expected people to do those things they could do about the situation before He would do those things for them that they could not do. He ordered paralytics to pick up their mats. He ordered people with withered limbs to extend their arms. He ordered people with leprosy to present themselves to the priests. He ordered blind people to go to the pool and rinse mud from their eyes.

Are you getting the point? God doesn't just sit on His throne, anxiously waiting for us to pray so He can jump into action to solve all our problems. God sits on His throne, anxiously waiting for us to do something to solve our own problems and the problems of those around us so He can jump into action and do the last step in the process for us, the part that we cannot do, the miraculous part. Miracles follow faithful service, and the power of the Holy Spirit always follows the bold and aggressive confrontation of human problems. That's why Jesus said, "These signs shall follow them that believe" (Mark 16:17, KJV). The signs don't come first; the signs *follow* something. They follow preaching. They follow service. They follow problem solving. Do you want to see more of the power of God in your life? More manifestations of the Holy Spirit's presence? Then get busy solving problems in the lives of other people.

We humans love titles. We love to be called "doctor" or "reverend" or "pastor" or any other title of respect. In the kingdom of God, however, none of these titles matter as much as the title of "servant." In fact, the highest position you can occupy in the kingdom of God is the position of a servant and the highest commendation you can receive on the Day of Judgment is the commendation, "Well done, good and faithful servant" (Matthew 25:23, KJV).

But what is a servant? In my way of thinking, a servant is somebody who solves problems. A servant has one or two responsibilities, not more, and he focuses all his time and creative energy on solving problems for the one he serves. Perhaps his duties involve the care of his employer's lawn or the cleaning of his employer's house. If the servant's responsibilities include the care of the lawn, the employer expects that servant to do just that: take care of the lawn. When it needs mowing, the employer doesn't want to be concerned with that problem. He wants the servant to mow the lawn or have the lawn mowed by someone else. When a new lawn care tool is needed, the employer wants his servant to buy the best tool for the job, store the tool, and maintain the tool. When a particular pest or blight is discovered in a particular thatch of grass, the employer wants the servant to solve the problem and get rid of the invader. The employer doesn't want to be bothered with the problem. He wants the problem solved.

A servant is nothing more and nothing less than a problem solver, and, if you think about it, that's what any job boils down to. Your boss hired you to solve a particular problem for him. Either he doesn't have the time or he doesn't have the know-how to solve the problem himself. Regardless of the reason, your boss pays you money to solve problems for him. And as long as you continue to solve more problems than you create, you will have a job. This is exactly the way it is with the Lord and with His servants in the work of the kingdom. God has called us to be His servants by solving human problems on His behalf. In the end, we are either part of God's problem or we are part of His solution. To be part of His solution is to be His faithful servant and to solve problems.

In fact, this is how Jesus served, as we have seen. Jesus came to solve human problems on behalf of God. He showed us the way to do it. Even though you and I don't have the ability to walk on water or raise the dead, we do have the ability to seat people in organized groups, serve fish and bread, and dip water from a jar. So if we will just faithfully do those things the Lord has put in our hands to do, He has promised to do the rest. He has promised to do the part that we cannot do. He will definitely show up to perform the miraculous if we will show up to do the natural. He loves it when we get our hands dirty solving the problems of others.

Whenever you read the Bible, please notice that God never elevated anyone to a higher position of authority and responsibility until that person first learned to serve others on a lower level by solving their problems. Take Joshua as an example. We are formally introduced to Joshua in the very first sentence of the book that bears his name. In that sentence, we are told, "Now after the death of Moses the servant of the LORD it came to pass, that the LORD spake unto Joshua the son of Nun, Moses' minister, saying, Moses my servant is dead; now therefore arise, go over this Jordan, thou, and all this people, unto the land which I do give to them, even to the children of Israel" (Joshua 1:1-2, KJV). Notice how this mighty man of God is described. He is described, not as one of the two spies who gave a favorable report on the Promised Land (see Numbers 13). He is described, not as a military leader who successfully defended Israel against the attacks of her enemies (see Exodus 17:10). Joshua, who would become the new "head" of Israel and would lead Israel in the conquest of Canaan, was described by God as "Moses' minister."

That is what made Joshua worthy of leadership. That is what made him great. Joshua was a servant. But notice that he was not introduced as "God's minister," instead, he was introduced as "Moses' minister." All his life, Joshua had solved problems for Moses. He had made Moses' life better and easier. He had made Moses successful. So God elevated Joshua. When Joshua served the man of God, God counted it as service to the Lord. That's the way it remains to this day. When you serve other people by helping them solve their problems, God reckons that service to your account as if you had done it for Him personally. Consequently, when you give a cup of cold water to someone who is thirsty, thus solving their problem of thirst, God scores that act as if "ye have done it unto me" (see Matthew 25:37-40, KJV). When you visit someone who could use some companionship and encouragement, thus solving that person's problem of loneliness, God scores that act as if "ye have done it unto me." God keeps score really well, but He counts everything you do for others and every problem you solve for other people as if you did if for Him personally.

SOLVING PROBLEMS FULFILLS YOUR
PURPOSE AND DESTINY IN THE WORLD

I cannot tell you how many people I have met who tell me they are praying for God to reveal to them their respective roles in life. All people need a purpose for their lives. All people need a destiny. All people need significance, worth, and a sense of importance. But I believe the best way to find your destiny is by getting involved solving problems for others. Just look around you and find a need that you can fill, then fill it. I promise you that, if you haven't already found your unique calling in life, you will find it as you go about solving problems for others.

Just look at the list of gifts and ministries that God enumerates in the Bible. Just look at the list of special gifts God has given to men. The Bible tells us that God destined "some to be apostles, some to be prophets, some to be evangelists, and some to be pastors and teachers" (Ephesians 4:11). The Bible also tells us that He has given one person "the message of wisdom, to another the message of knowledge by means of the same Spirit, to another faith by the same Spirit, to another gifts of healing by that one Spirit, to another miraculous powers, to another prophecy, to another distinguishing between spirits, to another speaking in different kinds of tongues, and to still another the interpretation of tongues" (I Corinthians 12:8-10). But if you think about it, all these ministries and manifestations of the Spirit are nothing more than divine appointments to solve problems for other people. Teachers teach people things they do not know and answer lingering questions for them as they help people learn the principles of God's kingdom and ways of applying those principles in their everyday lives. Evangelists engage people who have no spiritual life and inspire them to accept God's gift of eternal life. People with the gift of faith have an anointing to motivate people to look beyond the immediate problem to God's long-term solution. And people who can discern spirits have a powerful ability to protect their homes, their churches, and those under their influence from harmful influences.

God doesn't need anything from us. Yes, He desires our praise, but He won't perish if He doesn't get it. When you really think about it, God doesn't need anything we have or anything we can give Him. Apart from worship, there is nothing He really *wants* from us. There is nothing we have that can really benefit God in any way. God doesn't get hungry, so He doesn't need our food. God doesn't buy things, so He doesn't need our money. God doesn't get lonely, so He doesn't need our time. God doesn't get sad, so He doesn't need our comfort and encouragement. God doesn't need anything. He is self-sufficient. But the people He loves need all kinds of things. They need attention and affection and assurance and assistance. They need hope and help and honor and happiness. So God has come up with the most wonderful way to make everything fit. He uses you and me to solve the problems and meet the needs of others. He takes the credit for our efforts, so we won't become conceited. Then He gives us rewards for doing these things in His place. Even though most of the rewards will be distributed in heaven, He gives out some of those rewards right now in the form of favor.

SOLVING PROBLEMS BRINGS THE FAVOR OF MAN, AS WELL AS THE FAVOR OF GOD

When you and I help someone solve a problem, we use our God-given talents to do God's work on His behalf and in His name. Consequently, we procure the favor of God in this life and the approval of God in eternity. But by helping others solve their problems, we also procure the favor of the people we bless. Remember, "Jesus grew in wisdom and stature, and in favor with God and men" (Luke 2:52). Nothing brings the favor of man quite like solving problems for man.

Just think about it! Why did Joseph become the second-most powerful man in Egypt? Obviously, Joseph prospered because God had made a promise to him and because God showed him favor throughout his lifetime. But from a practical perspective, what was it that caused Pharaoh to decide to elevate Joseph to such a lofty and noble position? Pharaoh elevated Joseph because Joseph solved a problem for Pharaoh. Just as Joseph had solved a problem for Potiphar by taking care of his estate and causing him to prosper (thus bringing Potiphar's favor upon him) and just as Joseph had solved a problem for the chief jailer by organizing and managing the prison for him, making him look good in Pharaoh's eyes (thus incurring the jailer's favor upon his life), so Joseph solved a problem for Pharaoh. Joseph interpreted a recurring dream that nobody else could interpret, a dream that was driving Pharaoh insane. Then Joseph spelled out for Pharaoh exactly what he must do in response to the dream, so Pharaoh honored Joseph by showing him favor.

The same pattern occurs throughout the Bible. Nebuchadnezzar favored Daniel because Daniel solved problems for him. Artaxerxes favored Nehemiah because Nehemiah solved problems for him. Moses favored Joshua because Joshua solved problems for him. God has given certain people the ability to enrich your life. Some of them can bless you financially. Some of them can promote you professionally. Some of them can catapult you academically. Some of them can get you things at a reduced cost or introduce you to people you need to meet or open doors of opportunity for you that you could never open by yourself. If you can learn to solve problems for these people and for other people that these people know, you will incur their favor and make the pathway of your life much smoother and much easier to travel. God has promised to pour out His blessings upon your life, but He has promised to deliver His blessings through the hands of people (see Luke 6:38). You need to inspire people of means to look upon you favorably so they will allow God's blessings to flow through their hands into yours.

Solving Problems Glorifies the Lord

Here's a simple truth: You are either part of God's problem or you are part of God's solution. So which will it be? At one time, when you were lost in sin, you were definitely part of God's problem. You were the reason His Son had to die on the cross. You were the cause of much emotional pain for those who loved you. You were, in some ways, a burden to society. You were the inspiration for many prayers as other people lifted your name to God. But now that you are saved, God wants you to turn that around. He wants you to become part of His solution for the world. He wants you to give more than you receive. He wants you to forgive at least as much as you have been forgiven. He wants you to help others achieve their destinies, just as Joshua helped Moses achieve his destiny. He wants you to make life easier, better, more fulfilling, and more enjoyable for the people around you. He wants you to pluck lost souls from the flames of hell. He wants you to inspire and motivate those who look up to you.

When you do what God has created you to do, you become an answer for many of man's problems. You become a solution for many of man's dilemmas. You add more than you subtract. You contribute more than you take. In return, God is pleased to favor you. He is pleased to elevate you and to show you His goodness. When you do good things for others, especially when you do them in the Lord's name, God will honor you and elevate you and He will let the whole world know that you are special in His eyes. Nothing glorifies God more than your obedient attention to that which is most important to Him, and that which is most important to Him are the people who need His love and care. So love people as God would love them by doing everything you can do to meet their legitimate needs and solve their legitimate problems. Then God, in turn, will bless you. Everyone has problems. The favor you receive will depend on the willingness you have to solve problems for others.

Now that I have clearly demonstrated the centrality of problem solving to the Christian life, let me get practical for a moment. Let me conclude my thoughts on this matter by sharing with you four practical things you can do to solve problems for other people. Remember, by doing these things you will incur more of God's favor for your own life.

1. SOLVE PROBLEMS BETTER THAN ANYONE ELSE

I know a particular lady who does alterations better than anyone I know. She listens to me and does exactly what I ask her to do, and, over the years, she has learned to read my mind. This woman knows exactly what I like when it comes to my alterations, and she knows exactly how to make me happy, even when I fail to adequately explain my needs to her.

Because of the nature of my work, I buy a lot of clothes, and sometimes I buy those clothes in other cities or states. I even buy clothes overseas, but I never allow the people who sell me these clothes to alter the clothes for me, even if the alterations are included in the purchase price. Instead, I bring the clothes home and let my friend do all the alterations. Then I pay her over and above what she normally charges. Why? Because she does alterations better than anyone I know.

This lady doesn't run a sewing business; she runs a "problem solving" business. She solves problems for people who need alterations, and she solves those specific problems better than anyone else. With this approach to her work, she will never go hungry. People will beat a pathway to her door, if necessary, and her reputation will always precede her. She will never lack respect. She will never lack appreciation and praise. God will favor her through the people who come to her with their problems, problems that find their direct fulfillment in the special talent that God has given to her.

2. SOLVE PROBLEMS FASTER THAN ANYONE ELSE

People will pay more money for Internet service that gives them faster connections. People will pay more money for CD's that teach them a foreign language faster than those of other providers. People will frequent any business that will wash their car faster or get them into the dentist's chair faster or get them out the door with their hamburger and fries faster than anybody else. But people won't long endure a business or an employee who drags his feet and takes too long to do the simplest things.

Our country has become the fastest-paced country in the world. We want everything done with excellence, and we want it done this moment. But that's not altogether a bad thing. Our nation's thirst for speed and excellence has, in many ways, improved the quality of life for all of us. Obviously, some things can't be rushed, and I believe that all reasonable people understand this. Also, some things improve in quality when they are done more slowly and deliberately. People understand this too. But for the most part, those who figure out a faster way to get from here to Winslow or a faster way to make paint dry or a faster way to ship packages from Biloxi to Pine Grove are those who will incur the respect and loyalty of the buying public. Never sacrifice quality and never do your work with haste, but do learn to work with alacrity. There's no reason to take longer on a job than is necessary.

Have you ever been in a hurry to get somewhere only to find yourself driving on a one-lane highway behind a very slow pickup truck? This happens to me a lot on some of the back roads of Florida. Usually, these slow-moving trucks have one or two men in them who are obviously traveling somewhere to work. Probably, they are traveling from one job site to another. I can almost assure you that these workers are employees of someone else and that they work for an hourly wage, because if they worked for themselves or if they were paid by the job instead of the hour, they would be driving much faster. I understand that a lot of people are overworked and that a lot of people are in too big of a hurry to finish complicated tasks, but I don't think this is nearly the problem that slowness and procrastination are. In our society, we are programmed to be paid by the hour and to do as little as possible during that hour. Why should we work harder for the same amount of money? This mentality, though typical, is not pleasing to God.

God expects our best, and He rewards us for our best. He also expects our optimum output. People understand that *more* is usually better than *less*. This is why people frequent restaurants that get their food to them faster and body shops that can get the parts in faster. This also is why employers eventually reward those who get more done in a day. People don't like to wait unnecessarily.

3. SOLVE PROBLEMS WITH A GOOD ATTITUDE

Attitude is probably as important as the task itself and equally as important as the speed with which a task is performed. Think about it! Would you prefer to hire somebody who whistles while he works or someone who whines and complains the whole time he is working, and then grumbles to everybody after he is finished? The truth is that people will put up with a lot of "junk" in order to get good work done and they will put up with a lot more "junk" in order to get good work done quickly. But eventually, the quality and the quantity of the work won't matter if the customer or the boss has to listen to constant bellyaching the whole time. In fact, I wouldn't want Michelangelo to paint my house if I had to listen to him whine and complain the whole time. I might endure his bad attitude or avoid him altogether while he puts on the first coat of paint, but I would hire somebody else to put on the second coat.

Top executives, including senior pastors of large churches, will tell you that attitude is one of the most important things they consider when they are interviewing new prospects for an important position. People with excellent attitudes are the first associates these executives promote to positions inside their inner circles. No person of greatness wants to be near a person with a bad attitude. A person with great ambitions wants to be around people who will emulate his good qualities and make up for his bad ones with their own positive contributions. Consequently, a person who can keep a good attitude in the midst of adversity or a person who can remain cool and calm in a hostile environment is the person the boss will respect and the person he will promote.

We have all heard it before: Your attitude determines your altitude. This is absolutely true. No matter how much talent God has given to you, you will never rise higher than your attitude.

4. ALWAYS BE WILLING TO SOLVE
A PROBLEM FOR SOMEONE ELSE

At some point in your life, I am sure you have heard somebody say, "That's not in my job description." Maybe so! Perhaps that is *not* in your job description, but the person who does only what is expected of him and nothing more is the person who will never prosper and never receive God's favor in his life. This person embodies mediocrity. In fact, this sentiment is the very definition of mediocrity, and, as we saw in the previous chapter, mediocrity is not the spirit or climate of heaven and it is not the attitude of a child of God.

Those who would follow Christ are those who must be willing to "go the extra mile." They are the ones who must be willing to take up the cross, lay down their own lives, and perform the will of God with unbridled passion. The will of God is not some mysterious thing out there in the far-distant future, and it is not an adventurous excursion halfway around the world in some exotic mission field in a land of thatched huts. The will of God is that which the Lord has placed in front of you today. It is the responsibilities that are in your hand right now. The will of God is your job. The will of God is your family. The will of God is your church, your school, and your community. If you can't be faithful with the little things that God has placed in your hands today, you will never be faithful with the fantasy film that plays in your head about preaching to multitudes or pioneering new churches in unreached lands. And if you can't be faithful with the things God has given you to do during this season of your life, He will never trust you with more during later seasons. You also will miss out on many expressions of God's divine favor.

If you truly want to see God's favor increase in your life, you will have to make yourself available to the Lord every day of your life so He can use you whenever He wants and however He wants to do what needs to be done in the lives of the people around you. You will have to allow God to use you to improve the lives of your friends and loved ones, to solve the problems of your boss, and to ensure the growth and success of your church and the company where you work. In short, you will have to become God's hands to a world that desperately needs God's help. You will have to become a tool in God's hands for solving the problems of humanity.

Obviously, you can be saved without doing any of these things. Salvation doesn't depend on your works; it depends on your faith. But if you want to see God's favor in your life while you are still living in this present world, you are going to have to become aware of some foundational spiritual principles. One of those principles is that God honors those who honor Him. By placing yourself at God's disposal and by making yourself available to do God's work in the world, you bless the Lord, you bless others, and you make yourself a person God is pleased to elevate.

God favors those who pour themselves out upon others, especially when they are doing so to attract attention to the Lord instead of themselves. Look around you and become aware. Open your eyes and see the obvious. Wherever there are people, there are problems. And wherever there are problems, there are opportunities for serving God and for demonstrating His love and power to hurting individuals. Don't be a spectator; be a participant in life and in the work of God. Make yourself available to solve the problems of the people God has placed within your life. As you do, you will notice obvious increases in God's blessings and His favor.

CHAPTER 6
GIFT GIVING

BY GIVING A GIFT, YOU CAN
INCREASE FAVOR IN YOUR LIFE

Whenever the president of the United States visits another country, he takes gifts with him to present to the head of state of the nation he is visiting. Whenever another head of state visits the president in Washington, that world leader brings a gift, as well. Since the beginning of time, leaders have carried gifts with them when traveling to meet their counterparts around the world. Men of lower position have done the same thing when entering the presence of someone with greater authority. Gift giving has always been a part of initiating and building important relationships.

When the queen of Sheba visited King Solomon, for instance, she gave Solomon "120 talents of gold, large quantities of spices, and precious stones. Never again were so many spices brought in as those the queen of Sheba gave to King Solomon" (I Kings 10:10). In return, "King Solomon gave the queen of Sheba all she desired and asked for, besides what he had given her out of his royal bounty"

(I Kings 10:13). When Jacob sent his sons back to Egypt to meet personally with the right-hand man of Pharaoh in order to buy additional grain from him, Jacob sent his sons with "some of the best products of the land…a little balm and a little honey, some spices and myrrh, some pistachio nuts and almonds" (Genesis 43:11). And whenever an Israelite approached a prophet or a man of God to enlist that man's services, the Israelite would always take a gift with him (see I Samuel 9:7).

Gifts are great tokens for demonstrating one's respect. They also are great for breaking the ice with people you want to know or need to know. But above all, a gift can be extremely helpful in procuring favor for the one who gives it. Perhaps this is what Solomon meant when he wrote, "A gift opens the way for the giver and ushers him into the presence of the great" (Proverbs 18:16).

I can remember reading this verse of scripture and hearing people quote it when I was growing up in Mississippi. Like any young boy attending church, I was curious about the Scriptures and I wanted to understand what the Bible was saying to me. I also wanted to understand what this particular verse meant in the context of my modern culture. When I would ask about this verse, however, most of my teachers would tell me that this passage was referring to spiritual gifts. According to those who tried to explain the verse's meaning to me, Solomon was talking about God-given gifts and talents, and he was telling us that if we would use our talents for God, then God would promote us. He would open doors of opportunity for us by ushering us into the presence of great people, who would then promote us.

But that is not what this verse in Proverbs is saying. I know this is a book about favor, not about hermeneutics (the study of how to accurately interpret the Bible), nevertheless, I can tell you that the first rule of sound Bible study is to simply let the Bible speak for itself. Most of the time, the Bible says what it means and means what it says. We don't have to look any deeper. In fact, I am convinced that the single biggest problem most people have with the Bible is not that it is difficult to understand. To the contrary, the biggest problem most people have with the Bible is that it is far too easy to understand. We just don't want to believe what it tells us to believe and we don't want to do what it tells us to do, so we engage in all kinds of mental gymnastics in an effort to make the Bible say what we want it to say or what we think it should say, instead of what it actually says.

The Bible can never mean what it never meant. With the possible exception of some dual application passages in the prophetic books, all the language of the Bible must continue to mean what it originally meant to the human author who wrote it and to the people who were the original recipients of the text. To them, the meaning was not distorted at all; it was quite clear. And with this in mind, Solomon was quite clear when he wrote this little verse about giving gifts. As a king, he had received many gifts from his subjects and from other world leaders. He also had given many gifts to others, so he knew what he was talking about. He was talking about a literal, material, physical gift, not a "talent" or a "gift of the Spirit." Nobody living during the time of Solomon could have even known what a "spiritual gift" was.

Solomon was telling God's people of his day that if they could learn to give gifts to others, those gifts could have a profoundly positive impact on the people who received them and on their lives, as well. But this observation of human nature wasn't intended for just Old Testament believers; Solomon was making an observation that would apply to all people, everywhere, in every culture and in every generation. People enjoyed receiving gifts in China in 700 B.C. and people still enjoy receiving gifts in 21st-Century America. So the practice of gift giving still works today. In fact, the right gift given in the right way at the right time can open doors for you that you never thought could be opened. Your gift can even usher you into the presence of the great and the powerful. It can change your life.

Perhaps you have never thought about this, but throughout the Bible, God required people to enter His presence bearing gifts. In fact, He warned them never to enter His presence empty-handed. Whenever the Jews came to the temple to worship God, therefore, they would bring their sacrifices and offerings with them. When the high priest entered the Holy of Holies each year on the Day of Atonement (Yom Kippur), he would bear various bowls filled with incense or blood, and he would make several sacrifices before entering God's presence. Writing about the God of heaven, David said that we should, "Enter into his gates with thanksgiving, and into his courts with praise" (Psalm 100:4, KJV). In other words, even in this modern era when the blood of bulls and rams is no longer required and no longer appropriate, God still doesn't want us entering His presence empty-handed. He at least wants us to come into His presence with words of praise and gratitude.

Why does God require this from us? Because it is inappropriate to enter the presence of royalty without a gift! In fact, in the ancient Middle East, it was considered an insult to enter the presence of royalty without an appropriate gift. You could actually lose your head for entering the presence of a king without a worthy token of your esteem and respect. This sheds new light on the practice of gift giving at the birth of Christ. We are all familiar with the wise men and their gifts of gold, frankincense, and myrrh, but there are a lot of details about this story that most of us probably haven't discovered. It was no accident that God led these men on a long journey so they could take gifts to the Christ child. The giving of gifts was tantamount to affirming the royal lineage of the son of Joseph and Mary.

The Bible tells us that "when Jesus was born in Bethlehem of Judaea in the days of Herod the king, behold, there came wise men from the east to Jerusalem, saying, Where is he that is born King of the Jews? for we have seen his star in the east, and are come to worship him" (Matthew 2:1-2, KJV). The Bible doesn't tell us exactly how many of these wise men there were (though tradition tells us there were three), and the Bible doesn't tell us precisely where they came from or how long it took them to make the journey to Bethlehem. The truth of the matter is that these men probably came from Persia. The word *magi* is a Persian word meaning "wise men," and Persia was definitely in "the east." In addition, the primary religion of ancient Persia was Zoroastrianism, which involved the study of the stars and other heavenly bodies for the purpose of detecting prophetic signs of approaching earthly events.

At that time in history, Persia was home to the world's largest population of Jews - more Jews lived in Persia than in Israel itself because many Jewish families had remained there following the exile of 586 B.C. Because of this, the wise men were probably comfortable around Jewish people, and they probably were quite familiar with the prophecies of the Old Testament concerning the promised Messiah. They also kept their eyes on the stars, looking for signs of great world events. Because they were referred to as "wise men," they were probably counselors to the king or noblemen of some sort in their country.

The journey from Persia to Israel and back would have been a lengthy journey of several months, thus requiring these wise men to seek the blessing and permission of their king before making such a journey. It also means that it is highly unlikely that these men actually arrived in Bethlehem on the night when Jesus was born. It is much more probable that they arrived several months or even a year or more after the birth of Jesus, and this explains why Herod, after inquiring about the time when the star first appeared to them, decided to kill all the male children in Bethlehem under the age of two.

I am taking this wonderful, heart-warming story from the Bible and giving you this rather factual analysis of it to make a point: The wise men were not uncommon men. They were the elite of their society. They were the highest-ranking among their people. They were the most educated, most trusted, and most respected members of the upper class. They lived each day in the presence of their king. This is why when they traveled to see Jesus, they carried gifts with them. They knew the inappropriateness of entering the presence of royalty without a gift. To enter the presence of a king without an appropriate gift was to invoke the wrath of the king and to bring judgment upon oneself.

When you bring a gift to God, you show Him, as the wise men did, that He is worth more to you than the thing you have given to Him. It demonstrates that you respect Him and that you respect His position in your life and His authority over your life. When the wise men brought their gifts to Jesus, the giving of those gifts also represented their time (months of travel), their personal inconvenience (leaving their homes, their families, and the king they served), their personal sacrifice (the trip was exhausting and physically dangerous), and their trouble (dealing with Herod was no piece of cake). But isn't this precisely what the New Testament tells us we should be willing to do for God, as well as for those people who are important to us? Doesn't Paul tell us to, "Honor one another above yourselves" (Romans 12:10)? And doesn't Peter tell us to, "Show proper respect to everyone" (I Peter 2:17)?

Whenever Christine and I travel to a church to minister there, it is not uncommon for us to take a gift with us for the senior pastor of the church. I want to make it clear, however, that we do not take the gift in order to manipulate the pastor. After all, we have already been invited to preach in his church, so it's not like we're trying to influence him in any way. Rather, we bring our gift with us in order to honor the man of God and to show our respect for his office and his valuable work. We also bring the gift to help us say "thank you" for the opportunity to minister to the people God has entrusted to his spiritual care. We want the pastor to know that we esteem his position very highly and we appreciate the battles he wages on the front lines of Christian service. While his ministry is much more in the trenches, our type of ministry often brings more accolades.

Please understand that, if you start giving gifts just to get something you want, you will have to continue giving gifts in order to continue with that relationship. Manipulating others through gift giving often means that you will have to allow them to manipulate you in return. The general rule of thumb is that friendship or honor acquired through manipulation must be maintained by manipulation. For this reason, never give gifts in order to get an immediate return on investment. Give gifts in order to honor those who are truly worthy of your gifts: people whose position demands your respect or people whose character or acts of service have inspired you. If you give gifts in order to honor the honorable or in order to thank the worthy, then you give them for the right reason.

In the end, people can discern the motives behind your actions, and this reminds me of a story about a king and two of his subjects. It seems that there was an old farmer who lived just outside the city where the royal palace stood, and this farmer raised vegetables that his wife and children would sell in the marketplace. One day, while harvesting his crops, the farmer pulled up some of the most beautiful carrots he had ever seen. The weather had been quite cooperative that year and the rainfall had been perfectly adequate. So the farmer gathered up a large supply of these carrots and headed for the palace. At the gate, he was stopped, and the guards asked him to state his business.

"I would like to give a gift to the king," the man said as he held up this beautiful handful of carrots. So the guards escorted the farmer into the palace, where he was actually allowed into the throne room to greet the king.

The king was a good king, and he was well respected and loved by his subjects. As the farmer approached the throne and bowed, the king asked him to identify himself and to state his business. The man declared his name and then held up his beautiful carrots. He said, "Your Majesty, I have labored on my farm outside the walls of our great city all my life, and these are the most beautiful carrots I have ever harvested. I wanted to bring them to you and present them to you as a token of my high regard for you and for the leadership you have provided for our people."

The king, sensing the sincerity of the farmer, rose from his throne and went down to personally accept the carrots from the hand of the man. He looked them over carefully and returned to his throne. Then he addressed the man in the presence of his court. He said, "Well done, good man. You definitely have a talent for growing the best vegetables. I seem to recall that I have a large tract of land just beside the farm that you and your family have owned for generations. I want to give you that land. In return for it, I ask you to supply me with a small portion of what you produce so I can stock my table each day with some of your wonderful produce. The rest of what you harvest will be yours, and the land will be yours and your family's from this day forward."

The man was astonished at the king's kindness and generosity. With tears in his eyes, he bowed to the ground and thanked the king. Then he departed.

In the audience that day was one of the king's noblemen, who was known for the quality horses he bred. Noticing the kindness of the king toward the simple farmer, this nobleman decided that he was going to take advantage of the king's generosity by bringing a gift of his own to the king. *I will give the king my finest horse,* the man thought to himself. *Surely the king will edify me in the presence of my peers and promote me to a much more suitable position.*

So the next day, the nobleman entered the courtyard of the palace, leading his finest stallion behind him. He bowed to the king and said, "Your Majesty, it has always been my highest honor to serve under your wise leadership and authority. As you know, like my father and his father before him, I have always raised the world's finest horses, and I would like to honor you today by presenting to you the most impressive stallion in my stable."

Sensing the nobleman's impure motives and remembering that the nobleman was present the day before when the farmer was highly rewarded for his genuine, heartfelt gift, the king approached the nobleman, took the reigns of the horse from his hand, and simply said, "Thank you!"

If you give gifts for the wrong reason, your efforts will always backfire on you. But if you give gifts for the proper reason and with the right intentions, people will honor you for it. God will honor you, too. As Solomon noted in the book of Proverbs, your gifts can open doors for you that no other "key" could possibly open. They can incur for you the favor of men that nothing else could ever earn. Blessing God and blessing other people by giving them gifts with a pure heart and pure motivations is a proven and reliable way to gain the attention of the Lord and earn the trust of those you love and admire. Learn to give more than you receive, and learn to give in ways that will cause people to acknowledge your character.

CHAPTER 7
SOWING SEED

By obeying God's laws of giving,
you will increase in favor

If you have been a Christian for any length of time, you are undoubtedly familiar with the directive of the prophet Malachi, who wrote:

Will a man rob God? Yet ye have robbed me. But ye say, Wherein have we robbed thee? In tithes and offerings. Ye are cursed with a curse: for ye have robbed me, even this whole nation. Bring ye all the tithes into the storehouse, that there may be meat in mine house, and prove me now herewith, saith the LORD of hosts, if I will not open you the windows of heaven, and pour you out a blessing, that there shall not be room enough to receive it.

Malachi 3:8-10 (KJV)

It is obvious from this text that the practice of tithing was designed by God to provide His people with an opportunity for blessing. God doesn't need our money. What could He possibly buy that He doesn't already have? Where could He possibly travel that He hasn't already been? What pleasurable experience could He possibly gain with tangible money? He is God. But God uses the grace of giving to test and build the faith of His people and to promote the work He has given His people to do in the world. In turn, He blesses those who demonstrate their faithfulness to Him through their giving.

In this final chapter, I want to draw a strong connection between the practice of giving by God's people and the outpouring of favor by God. In the Bible, these two activities are definitely connected, so let's take a look at what God has to say about our willingness to release our financial resources to Him and His resulting willingness to release His divine favor in our lives.

THE FOUNDATION OF ALL GIVING IS THE TITHE.

The word tithe is a biblical word that simply means "tenth" or "ten percent." To tithe is to faithfully give to God one-tenth of all one's increase, regardless of the form that increase may take. In the agrarian economy of the Old Testament, the Israelites typically brought a tenth of their produce to God when it was harvested, because, to the ancient Israelite, the produce of the land and the offspring of their flocks and herds represented their wealth. The people of Israel made a living by raising wheat and barley, cattle and sheep. These things and the products resulting from them would sustain the Israelites and their dependents and could also be sold in the marketplace for gold and silver, which could then be exchanged for other necessary products.

The Law of Moses commanded the Jews to bring to the Lord on a regular basis a tenth of all that their hands produced or to convert their produce to a monetary equivalent and then bring the money to the Lord. Actually, the Old Testament talks about three separate tithes: one tithe that was reserved for the Levites, who served in the house of the Lord (see Numbers 18:22-24); a second tithe of the produce of the land that was to be consumed by the family that produced it in a joyous ceremony of worship and thanksgiving at the house of the Lord (see Deuteronomy 14:22-27); and an additional tithe that was to be given every three years for the support of the fatherless, widows, and aliens who lived in the land (see Deuteronomy 14:28-29). To the Old Testament faithful, therefore, giving was a central part of their worship and it involved a lot more than just ten percent. Nevertheless, the foundation of all giving for them was the basic tithe, the first ten percent of a person's overall increase. This is still the basis for faithful giving today.

I realize that the subject of tithing is a touchy one for some people. There are many folks out there who, for various reasons, don't want to turn loose of their hard-earned cash. They love God, but either they are afraid to give away their money or they are offended by the fact that giving is mentioned so often in the context of their worship of God. They wish they could just enjoy God's benefits and not have to deal with the constant appeals by the church to support the work of the church with their giving. Consequently, some people spend a lot of time and do a lot of thinking in an effort to find plausible reasons not to give and to soothe their consciences because they don't give the way they are told they should. But I am not writing this chapter to rehash all the arguments for and against giving. I am writing this chapter simply to show you that giving is definitely linked to God's favor and to help you decide whether you want that favor or not.

Personally, it seems rather obvious to me that tithing is a *biblical* concept, not just an *Old Testament concept*, and I say this for two reasons. First, the most powerful biblical exhortation for tithing is the passage quoted above from the book of Malachi. I think the location of this exhortation is very important. If you will turn to Malachi 3:8-10 in your Bible, then turn the page just one more time, you will find that the New Testament starts on the very next page of your Bible. When God gave this tithing decree to Malachi to include in his prophetic writings to Israel, God knew that Malachi would be the last of the Old Testament prophets and that his book would be positioned last in the Hebrew Scriptures. If God had plans to do away with tithing in the New Testament, why would He wait until the very last page of the Old Testament to forcefully reinforce a practice that He intended to eliminate on the very next page?

I know that some people argue that tithing is not required in the New Testament, but I disagree. It doesn't make sense to me that God would strongly command His people to engage in a practice that would become obsolete as soon as they turned the page. If tithing were an Old Testament concept only, God would not have waited until the very end of the Old Testament to remind us of its centrality to worship; He would have called His people back to the practice of tithing much earlier in the Old Testament era.

It also seems obvious to me that Jesus practiced tithing. How do I know this? Can I quote a specific verse of Scripture that mentions Jesus tithing? No! But I believe the Scriptures tell us in an implicit way that Jesus practiced tithing when they describe for us the peculiar manner in which the Pharisees dealt with Jesus. Have you ever noticed how closely the Pharisees watched Jesus? If Jesus ate a kernel of corn on the Sabbath, the Pharisees made a federal case out of it. If Jesus ate a meal with someone who was ceremonially unclean, the Pharisees went hysterical. The religious elite of that day watched Jesus like a hawk watches a field, looking for any tiny thing they might exploit in order to discredit Him and His message. If Jesus had failed to tithe, don't you think the Pharisees would have mentioned that to the people, especially in light of the fact that Jesus encouraged them to tithe (see Matthew 23:23)?

The New Testament makes it clear that the Pharisees tithed and they tithed, not just their money, but their mint and dill and cumin. In other words, the Pharisees sat down and actually counted the leaves in their spice racks, giving a tenth of those leaves to God. That's how meticulous these people were about the Old Testament law. So if Jesus had failed to tithe according to the Law of Moses, the Pharisees definitely would have mentioned it.

Again, I don't want to turn this book into a defense of the doctrine of tithing, because I want this book to be about real life, not theology. Nevertheless, real life for the Christian is built upon a foundation of sound theology, so I am compelled to offer a basic theological foundation for tithing before I can show you the connection between giving and favor. Now that I have offered that foundation, I can tell you again what I told you before: giving is the fountain from which divine favor flows and tithing is the starting point for all giving. If you want to see the connection between giving and favor, just look at Solomon's admonition regarding giving, where he writes:

Honor the LORD with your wealth,
with the firstfruits of all your crops (your tithe);
then your barns will be filled to overflowing,
and your vats will brim over with new wine.
                    Proverbs 3:9–10 (parentheses mine)

The key word here is the word *then*. Honor the LORD with your wealth and with your tithe, THEN your barns will be filled,

THEN your vats will overflow. There is a cause and effect going on here. By giving, you invite the favor of God. By tithing, you open the channels of blessing in your life.

THERE IS AN IMPORTANT DIFFERENCE BETWEEN A TITHE AND AN OFFERING

According to the Bible, the tithe is the Lord's. It belongs to Him. He demands it because He views it as His rightful property and He truly believes that He has the right to claim it. According to Moses, "All the tithe of the land, whether of the seed of the land or of the fruit of the tree, is the LORD's. It is holy to the LORD" (Leviticus 27:30, NKJV). This is why the prophet Malachi could refer to the withholding of the tithe as robbery. You can only steal something that belongs to someone else; you cannot steal something that belongs to you. God has declared that the tithe belongs to Him.

When God, through the prophet Malachi, confronted the Jewish people about their neglect of tithing, He began His confrontation by asking the people a rhetorical question and by offering an answer to His own question. He asked, "Will a man rob God?" (Malachi 3:8, KJV). Then, He responded, "But ye have robbed me" (v. 8, KJV). Then God, still speaking through Malachi, proceeded to tell the people how to rectify this fault: He told them to "bring ye all the tithes into the storehouse" (v. 10, KJV).

To withhold God's tithe from Him, therefore, is to rob Him. If you are a Christian, the first ten percent of your increase (everything that is added to your life) belongs to the Lord. Once you begin to return to God the first tenth of all that He gives to you, you become a faithful tither. But this is not the end of the matter of giving, because the Bible also teaches us about "offerings."

Throughout the Old Testament, the people of God were encouraged to bring their freewill offerings to the Lord in addition to the tithes required from them. An offering is a gift of one's own resources or property. It is a gift from the heart that exceeds the expectations of God's fixed laws. To give God His tithe is simply to return to Him that which belongs to Him already. But to give God an offering is to give to Him something that belongs to you. So while the tithe is about faithfulness, offerings are about generosity. You cannot be generous with someone else's money, so giving God His own tithe is not an act of generosity. Giving God His tithe is an act of faithful obedience. It is returning to God His own property. But to give God an offering above and beyond His tithe is to truly demonstrate your love for Him and your generosity toward His work. It is a sacrifice on your part.

I have seen people withhold God's tithe. I personally know a Christian family that kept God's tithe and used it instead to buy a new car. I know of another believer who withheld God's tithe and used it to buy a new suit. I have watched these people drive their new cars to church and wear their new clothes into the sanctuary to worship God. I sometimes wonder if it has ever occurred to them that they are coming to church in a stolen car and that they are wearing stolen clothes, yet they lift their hands to worship the Lord.

My Bible says, "Thou shalt not steal" (Exodus 20:15, KJV). My Bible also says, "thieves… (shall not) inherit the kingdom of God" (I Corinthians 6:10, KJV). So when the prophet Malachi calls it "robbery" to withhold God's tithe from Him and use it instead for one's own purposes, I had better listen. Yet a lot of Christian people don't listen. They fail to heed these admonitions and they fail to connect these verses about tithing and stealing. They also fail to accept the fact that God's tithe belongs to Him and that keeping it for oneself is wrong. Are they so void of faith that they cannot trust God to meet their needs? Are they so materialistic that they will steal from someone who holds the power to judge them for their actions? Are they so unthankful for the ninety percent that God gives to them that they need to take the tiny little ten percent that God has set apart for Himself? I have never understood this mentality.

Not along ago, while ministering in a church, I asked the congregation, "When you bring your tithe, your ten percent to the Lord, how much do you have left?"

People throughout the sanctuary starting mumbling, "Ninety percent."

"That's not right," I responded. "Actually, you have 100 percent left. The ten percent was never yours in the first place. So you still have the entire amount that belongs to you."

God honors those who tithe. According to the promise He made in Malachi 3:8-10, God blesses those who tithe. But God especially blesses those who faithfully tithe and, at the same time, give Him offerings above and beyond His tithe. An offering is a gift of your own money, not God's. If you remember the things I wrote in the previous chapter, you will remember that gift giving is a pathway to divine favor and blessing. So do the math! If tithing brings God's blessing and favor and gift-giving brings God's blessing and favor, then bringing offerings to the Lord brings double blessing and double favor, because you have to tithe before you can give God a gift, and both tithing and gift-giving bring favor. The man who faithfully gives tithes and offerings, therefore, is a man who is truly blessed of the Lord.

Tithing, like nothing else, demonstrates the true level of one's faith

I'm trying hard not to be mean in this chapter. I'm just not a mean guy. At the same time, however, I want to be faithful to God's Word and I want to be honest with you. I have a problem when somebody tells me they have faith, yet they do not tithe and they do not give offerings to the Lord. I listen to all their excuses and to all their theological arguments for not giving to God, but deep down inside, I know the real reason people don't give: Either they are greedy and they want to keep all their material wealth for themselves, or they are afraid that their security might be jeopardized or their standard of living might suffer if they part with their hard-earned money.

Is this faith? How can a man say that he trusts God if he is afraid he won't make it in life without stealing God's money? How can a man claim to love God if he doesn't do anything to support the work of God in the world? But it goes deeper than that. I find it amazing that Christians can lift their hands and worship God with tears in their eyes whenever they sing about the promise of heaven or the power of the Lord to heal or deliver, yet these same people have a difficult time trusting God with the simplest needs of their everyday lives. How can a person trust God to raise his decaying body from the grave when he cannot trust God to put food on his table? How can a man trust God to fulfill hundreds of Bible prophecies regarding the end times when he cannot trust God to put shoes on his feet or a roof over his head? How can a woman trust God to save her immortal soul when she cannot trust God to meet her daily needs? How can an individual trust God to break the power of sin *in* his life when he cannot trust God to break the power of poverty *over* his life?

135

I could argue with you all day about your need to tithe and I could present you with dozens of reasons why you need to give offerings above your tithe, but when all is said and done and when the smoke clears and the dust settles and when all the destruction from the theological debate has been cleared away, there are really only two reasons for giving–because you love God and because you trust Him. In fact, to give nothing at all calls your love and faith into question. It's that simple, yet it's that profound.

I believe that tithing, like nothing else, proves your faith in God's Word. When you write your tithe check every week and throw in an occasional offering to support the work of a particular missionary or to bless a guest speaker who has ministered at your church, those checks are your tangible evidence that you believe God and His Word. And nothing touches the heart of God like faith. I'm not saying that God will overlook your sins if you show faith in your life, but I am saying that God can work through a lot of stuff when you have faith. On the other hand, He can do very little in your life when you don't have faith.

Just look at the people in the Bible. Other than Jesus, you won't find any perfect people in the Bible. Abraham showed a lot of cowardice in his life and he often deceived people. Jacob (whose name was changed to Israel) was a liar and a con artist. Joseph had a vibrant ego. Moses had a raging temper. Paul wasn't very patient with people (like Mark). Peter was renowned for putting his foot in his mouth and for being hypocritical at times. Nobody in the Bible was perfect, yet God used these people to part the seas, to raise the dead, to write the Scriptures, and to turn the world upside down with the Gospel. If they weren't perfect, what was it about their lives that captured God's attention and procured God's favor? What was it that set them apart from "mere men"? It was their faith. They believed

God. They knew how to trust God and that quality caused God to elevate them highly above their peers and to use them in spectacular ways to change the course of human history.

God loves faith, and God responds to faith. So when we show faith by relinquishing to God the money that we think we need to pay our light bills or our insurance premiums, that shows God how very much we love Him, how very highly we esteem His work, and how genuinely we trust Him. Yet when we fail to honor God with His tithes and our offerings, we say to Him in a loud and clear voice that we just do not believe Him or trust Him. Sure, Lord, we believe You for our salvation. And sure, Lord, we believe that You are coming back one day in the far-distant future to raise our bodies from the dead. Yes, Lord, we believe that You are building this magnificent kingdom for us in a place called heaven. But Lord, we just can't trust You to meet our monthly mortgage payments unless we keep Your tithes and use that money to provide for our own needs. We're just not sure that You can handle that responsibility, so we'd rather take care of those things ourselves, just to be on the safe side!

According to Malachi's promise in the Old Testament (see Malachi 3:8-10) and according to the promise of Jesus in the New Testament (see Luke 6:38), God's favor follows those who give because giving is an overt act of faith. At the same time, the reciprocal is true. Withholding God's tithe and withholding your offerings to Him brings God's disfavor and a curse. Malachi told the Jews who had forsaken the practice of tithing, "Ye are cursed with a curse" (Malachi 3:9, KJV). Moses told the people of God that, "if thou wilt not hearken unto the voice of the LORD thy God, to observe to do all his commandments and his statutes which I command thee this day (including tithing); that all these curses shall come upon thee, and overtake thee" (Deuteronomy 28:15, KJV, parentheses mine).

So be faithful with your giving and be regular with it. Paul said that believers should lay aside their tithes and offerings "upon the first day of the week" (I Corinthians 16:2, KJV). If you will give regularly and systematically to the work of the Lord, you will find that God responds to your faith by pouring out His blessings upon you and by flooding your life with His favor. Then your faith will grow even more, and your life will be blessed spiritually, as well as materially.

FAITHFUL GIVING ENGENDERS DIVINE FAVOR IN TWO WAYS

There are two ways to improve the water levels in a barrel. You can improve a barrel's water levels by pouring more water into the top of the barrel, and you can improve a barrel's water levels by closing the spigot at the bottom of the barrel. The contents of a barrel are enhanced both by adding to them and by slowing down the rate at which the barrel's contents are lost. Similarly, through the prophet Malachi, God promised to improve the financial posture of faithful givers in two ways: He promised to open the windows of heaven and pour out a blessing from above, and He promised to rebuke the devourer who consumes from below. By doing these two things, God shows His favor to us and improves the bottom line of our financial lives.

All of us understand the first promise of God through Malachi. When God says, "I will... open you the windows of heaven, and pour you out a blessing, that there shall not be room enough to receive it" (Malachi 3:10, KJV), we know what that promise means. It means that God wants us to give and that He will give back to us in abundance if we do give. He will increase our salaries. He will promote us on our jobs. He will bring new streams of income into our lives. He will open new doors of financial opportunity to us. He will cause our investments to give us a good return. He will do what Jesus promised: He will cause men to "give into your bosom" and to do so with "good measure, pressed down, and shaken together, and running over" (Luke 6:38, KJV).

So we understand this part of the blessing. It makes perfect sense. If we give to God, God will get directly involved in our lives and He will give back to us. He will give more to us than we give to Him. Got it! But the second part of God's promise in Malachi is sometimes overlooked. God promised not only to pour out His blessings from above, but also to fix the leaks from below that tend to drain our financial resources. He promised to "rebuke the devourer for your sakes" (Malachi 3:11, KJV).

Just think about this for a moment! How much money would you save over the course of your life if nothing ever went wrong in your life? Your refrigerator never needed repairs. Your car lasted a million miles. The shoes on your feet never needed resoling. Your garage door opener never needed replacing. Your computer never got a virus. Your children never got the measles or the mumps and they earned full scholarships to college. Your house never needed a new roof and your pickup truck never needed new tires. Obviously, I'm not going to tell you that you can walk in so much favor that nothing ever goes wrong in your life. That's just not biblical, and it's not practical either. As I said earlier in this book, life is problematic. You have been put here to solve problems, including your own problems. Nevertheless, I do know this: I do know that, with God's favor, a person can certainly experience supernatural intervention that noticeably decreases the negative occurrences in his life.

God made the shoes to last on the feet of the Israelites for 40 years while they wandered through the desert. He made the clothes on their backs last the same amount of time. If God can cause clothes and shoes to last for 40 years in a hostile environment, He can make your air conditioner last just a little bit longer and He can keep you from spending unnecessary amounts of money to keep your car running or to keep pests off your lawn. In short, He can "rebuke the devourer for your sakes."

If you enter into a financial covenant with God and keep your end of that agreement by regularly returning God's tithe to Him and routinely honoring Him with additional offerings, God has promised to get personally involved in your financial affairs. He has promised to stand guard over your life, your money, and your possessions. Although He won't cause physical things to last forever, He can supernaturally extend their usefulness and their life. He also can keep people from ripping you off or shortchanging you in any way. He can lead you to honest businessmen, to capable handymen, and to knowledgeable advisors who can save you a lot of money over the long haul.

But if you fail to be financially faithful to God, the prophet Malachi has made it clear that God will refuse to fight your financial battles for you. Things will go wrong at a faster pace. The leak in the bottom of your barrel will grow larger and larger, eventually causing everything you earn during the day to drain out of your life during the night while you sleep. No matter how much you pour into the top of your barrel, your barrel will never be full and you will be forced to work harder and harder just to keep the water levels at a safe place. You will put money in, but your barrel will always have a slow leak that you just can't seem to find. There will be holes in your pockets.

So God asks us to honor Him in two ways: by returning His tithe to Him and by giving Him our offerings. In return, He promises to favor us in two ways: by pouring out blessings from above and by sealing up the leaks below.

OUR TITHES AND OFFERINGS PRODUCE
GOOD THINGS IN THE WORLD

Can you imagine a world without churches? The spiritual needs of individuals would not be served, the Gospel would not be effectively proclaimed, and human life would sink to the level of mere biological survival. In all corners of the globe, evil would prevail, and there would be no voice of morality or beacon of light anywhere in the world.

It is God's tithe that makes the church possible, because God, in His infinite wisdom, has chosen to place the responsibility for His work in the hands of mortal human beings. He has entrusted us with the responsibility for building His house and for carrying out His commission to reach the lost for Christ.

Just as I have a problem with people who use our highways and national parks without paying taxes, so I have a problem with people who enjoy the benefits of our churches without helping to pay the churches' bills. I can understand why visitors and unchurched people don't give during the offering, but I don't understand how mature Christians can go to church and complain about the cleanliness of the facility or the efficiency of the air conditioning when they don't give anything to help pay for those services they expect.

Your tithes and offerings pay the salaries of those who serve the spiritual needs of God's people. Your tithes and offerings pay for the structures in which God's people gather. Your tithes and offerings pay the utilities that sustain those structures and for the various ministries that are conducted inside the structures' walls. And your tithes and offerings pay for the supplies, services, and expenses necessary to conduct the ministry activities that take place outside the walls of your church. In short, your tithes and offerings are the fuel that drives the engines of ministry. Without your faithful giving, there won't be any funds for printing, for curriculum, for insurance, for electricity, or for the support of the men and women who do the full-time work of ministry.

But faithful giving doesn't just benefit the church and the community that reaps the church's services. Faithful giving also benefits the one who gives in at least two ways. First, giving forces the giver to establish priorities in his life. All of us know that there is never enough money to do everything we want to do, so we are forced to establish priorities simply because money is a finite resource. Most of these priorities are no-brainers. They do not involve a lot of thought. It's obvious that we are going to buy food before we buy a new over-the-top cell phone. It's obvious that we are going to pay the mortgage before we pay the membership dues at the country club. No person has enough money to do everything that pops into his head or to buy everything the television commercials tell him he needs, so we learn as we are growing up that we need to prioritize our expenditures and the most important priorities get our foremost financial attention. When we give to God, therefore, we show Him that He is a high priority in our lives. We cherish Him more than a new set of golf clubs. We love Him more than we love vacationing in the Caribbean. We desire Him more than we desire a new Beamer or a new mink coat.

Some people would have you believe that, if you will give to God, God will give you everything that your heart could ever desire. In fact, people who believe this tend to "bait" others to tithe with the hope that they also can manipulate God into giving them things. But this premise isn't true. It's not smart either. If God met every desire of your heart, then giving would become meaningless and empty. It would lose its "worship" aspect, because it would no longer cost you anything. When you worship someone or something, you place great worth upon that person or object. The object of your worship is something you value very highly. So when you deny yourself and give to God, you show that you value God more highly than your own desires and appetites. You place greater worth on Him than you place on life's pleasures and things. This touches the heart of God and elicits favor from Him. But there is no favor without sacrifice. There is no reward without cost.

Sir, how does your wife know that you love her? Ma'am, how does your husband know that you love him? Because you demonstrate your love by placing that person's needs above your own! Sometimes, that involves the way you use your money. Sir, if you are constantly buying things for yourself while never spending a dime on your wife, how does that make her feel? It certainly doesn't make her feel loved, and it doesn't make her feel very valuable either. Ma'am, if you are always thinking of yourself and what you can get out of your marriage, but you never buy your husband a gift or do anything special for him, not even on his birthday, how do you think that is going to affect your marriage over the long haul? The way you spend your money tells everyone where your heart is. You spend your money on that which is important to you, because you will never have enough money to do everything you can think of doing. If you are always praying to God, asking Him for things, but you never give Him anything in return for His goodness to you, how do you think He interprets that? Do you think your worship perhaps falls on deaf ears?

Give me ten minutes of uninterrupted time to look through a person's check ledger and credit card statements, and I can tell you everything about that person you would ever want to know. I can learn more in ten minutes from a man's check ledger and credit card statements than a psychologist could learn in a thousand hours of therapy. I could discover all that person's fears. I could learn about that person's dreams. I could learn about all his priorities, what is important to him and what is unimportant. I could learn about his temptations and stumbling blocks. Why? Because you only have a limited amount of money, and where you put that money tells me what is important to you! Are your children important to you? Then your credit card statements will tell me so. Is your husband or wife important to you? Your friends? Your church? Then your check ledger will tell me so.

If I find nothing there to demonstrate that God is important in your life, then He probably isn't that important to you, and that may explain the lack of divine favor in your life. Your money will follow your heart and will manifest your true nature to God and to the people around you. The way you make your money and the way you spend your money will say more about you than anything else in life.

In Second Samuel 24, God struck the nation of Israel with a terrible plague and King David decided to make a special sacrifice to God to elicit His mercy in the situation. Over the previous three days, approximately 70,000 Israelites had died in the plague because of God's wrath against David. Under these circumstances, the prophet Gad told David that he should make his offering in a specific place, on the threshing floor of a man named Araunah. So David approached Araunah and offered to buy his threshing floor. When David made his offer, however, Araunah responded with a counteroffer: He offered to give the king the property at no cost, and he offered to throw in the oxen and anything else the king needed for free. But David declined Araunah's kind offer, telling him, "No, I insist on paying you for it. I will not sacrifice to the LORD my God burnt offerings that cost me nothing" (II Samuel 24:24, NIV).

Even for a king, money is not an endless resource, and David knew that sacrifice only has significance when it is truly a sacrifice. For this reason, parting with your hard-earned money in order to give it to God demonstrates faith in God's ability to take care of you. But perhaps more importantly, it demonstrates through actions (which always speak louder than words) that you place great value on God himself. You are giving up money you could use for another purpose in order to spend it extravagantly on the Lord, and you are doing this in much the same way that the woman extravagantly poured her very expensive perfume over the head of Jesus (see Matthew 26:6-7). The man who "wastes" his resources on God is the man who has firmly established his personal list of priorities, and God is at the top of his list. How do we know? Because this man had to remove something else from his list in order to make room for God! So faithful giving is the best way I know to put God first in your life and to keep Him there.

Second, faithful giving delivers us from the deadly sin of materialism. Giving, unlike any other activity, has a way of removing "things" from the throne of our hearts so God can reclaim His rightful place in our lives.

God doesn't have a problem with His people owning things; God just has a problem with things owning His people. I believe that God is inclined to give more things to people who can handle those things by keeping them in their proper subordinate role. I am equally convinced that God is less likely to entrust a lot of things to people who cannot handle those things. A person who is materialistic or hung up on image or made to feel secure when he is surrounded by a lot of "stuff" is the person God cannot trust with greater resources, because a person like this will fall deeper and deeper into the bottomless pit of materialism and may never be able to climb back out. Giving, therefore, is God's remedy for this terrible human malady. If you faithfully give to God in proportion to His blessing upon your life, God will be more inclined to trust you with additional money and more stuff. But if you cherish "things" more than you cherish God, the Lord is not going to reward you or subject you to more temptation. God will give you all that you can handle, but He will never give you more than you can bear.

Do you remember the parable about the master and his three servants? The master of the house was preparing to go on a long journey, but before leaving on this extended trip, he entrusted to his servants five talents, two talents, and one talent respectively (see this parable in Matthew 25:14-30). When the master eventually returned home, he found that the first two servants had been faithful stewards with the money placed under their care. They had invested the money given to them, doubling the talents for their master. But the third servant did nothing with the money the master had entrusted to his care, so the master stripped him of his single talent and threw him out of his house.

There are several lessons to be learned from this parable. We can learn, for instance, that money is a great tool for discovering people's motives, abilities, and priorities. We also can learn that God holds us accountable for what we do with His money and our money (or fail to do with it). We can also learn that people have different capacities for handling money. While some people handle money wisely and faithfully, others handle it poorly. This is why God tests us with money. By blessing us with financial resources and then watching what we do with those resources, the Lord learns the makeup of our hearts. He learns our strengths and our weaknesses. He learns the true level of our faith. This gives Him the working knowledge He needs when we kneel in prayer to petition Him for additional financial blessing. If we have been faithful with little, God will be more inclined to trust us with much. But if we have shown signs of materialism and selfishness, God won't be so inclined to pour His precious resources into our lives. Tithing, therefore, is God's cure for selfishness and materialism, just as it is His cure for a life without priorities.

LIKE NOTHING ELSE, TITHING PROVES THE RELIABILITY OF GOD

Only once in the entire Bible did God ever say, "Prove me." This is that one occasion. Through the prophet Malachi, God told the Israelites to "prove me now herewith, saith the LORD of hosts, if I will not open you the windows of heaven, and pour you out a blessing, that there shall not be room enough to receive it. And I will rebuke the devourer for your sakes, and he shall not destroy the fruits of your ground; neither shall your vine cast her fruit before the time in the field, saith the LORD of hosts" (Malachi 3:10-11, KJV).

Several years ago, when I was a senior pastor in Florida, I would periodically teach my congregation the principle of tithing. Once when I was teaching on this subject, I remember sharing with my church this same challenge that God put to the Jews through Malachi when He basically said: "Look, if you don't believe Me, just try it.

Put Me to the test. If tithing doesn't work, you will know it doesn't work from your own personal experience. But it does work. And what you are going to learn by putting Me to the test is that I will open the windows of heaven and pour out a blessing that you won't even have room to receive. Then I am going to take things a step farther. I am going to rebuke the devourer for you and plug up the leaks in the bottom of your barrel. You're actually going to be better off financially by giving Me My rightful portion of your income than you would be if you kept it. Don't believe Me? Just try it and see!"

I challenged my church to put God to the test. I gave them the same "deal" that God gave to the Israelites. I told them to try tithing for 90 days. "Do it faithfully, and do it consistently and with a cheerful heart, then see what happens," I said. "If God shows you His favor, then keep doing it. But if tithing doesn't work for you after 90 days of sincere effort, let me know and I will refund your money."

Do you know how many people wanted their money back after 90 days? Not one! A lot of people took me up on my offer to prove God, but nobody took me up on my offer to refund their money if He failed them, because He didn't fail them. In fact, the opposite took place. People who had never tithed before that challenge began to step forward to share personal testimonies about God's goodness to them in response to their step of obedience and faith. Most of these people had a shocked look on their faces as they told their stories, as if they weren't expecting God's promise to work for them.

I want to extend the same challenge to you. If you are not a tither, start tithing today. You can worry about adding your offerings later, but start by giving God that portion of your income which rightly belongs to Him anyway. After all, He gave you the skills and intelligence that you use to earn your daily bread. He gave you the health you need to work. He brought the people into your life who have been instrumental in your education and career. He blesses the business where you work and the industry you serve so there will be a demand for your skills and enough profits to justify your employment. Show Him how much you appreciate Him by giving Him the portion that rightly belongs to Him. Then watch what He does in your life. See if He doesn't open the windows of heaven and pour out a blessing on you that you cannot contain.

While we're talking about blessings that cannot be contained, I must admit that I haven't had the blessing yet that I cannot contain. This can only mean that God has more blessings for me that I haven't received yet. It must mean that I haven't fully tapped into all the benefits that are reserved for me as a faithful giver. But the blessings I have received already have been tremendous and obvious, so I intend to keep on giving and to keep looking to God as my source and my supply with an expectation of even greater blessing. I hope you will follow me.

A man with an experience is never at the mercy of a man with an opinion. I have the personal experience of tithing and watching God fulfill His promises to pour His favor into my life. So when people approach me with an opinion that tithing doesn't work because it doesn't make sense to their natural minds, I just laugh to myself. These poor people don't know what they're talking about. Like those spiritually blind people who cannot "see" that there is a God and that He loves them, these spiritually blind people cannot "see" that giving actually *increases* one's financial resources rather than diminish them. Don't believe me? Just try it. Don't believe what God has said about giving in His Word? Just put Him to the test. Prove Him. He's up for the challenge, and He's not afraid of your skepticism.

THERE ARE THREE FIXED AND
IRREFUTABLE LAWS OF THE HARVEST

When Jesus walked the earth, teaching people about the kingdom of God and the kingdom of heaven, He had a formidable challenge on his hands. On the one hand, He wanted people to know the eternal principles of His kingdom and the fixed laws of His creation. On the other hand, how could He make the people understand things they had never seen or experienced? His dilemma was a little like the dilemma you and I might face if we were asked to explain the color red to a man who was born blind.

So Jesus used physical things to make spiritual points. To help people understand spiritual realities they had never experienced and to help them grasp spiritual concepts they had never contemplated, Jesus used things like clouds and children and fishing nets and mustard seeds. He used sheep and bread and water and light. I could not possibly count the number of times Jesus used the word *like* or the word *as* while He made comparisons between the physical things of earth and the eternal principles of heaven. He would say things like, "The kingdom of heaven is like yeast that a woman took and mixed into a large amount of flour until it worked all through the dough" (Matthew 13:33), or "The kingdom of heaven is like treasure hidden in a field. When a man found it, he hid it again, and then in his joy went and sold all he had and bought that field" (Matthew 13:44).

Jesus was able to use physical things to make spiritual points because the same God who created the *spiritual world* also created the *physical world*. Although the spiritual and material worlds are different in many respects, these two worlds are more alike than they are different. This is true because the same creative mind that formed the spiritual world also formed the physical world. Consequently, many of the same rules apply in both worlds. Nowhere is this more true than in the area of agriculture. The principles of harvest that work in the physical world also work in the spiritual world, because the laws of the harvest are the same in both the physical and spiritual worlds.

What are the fixed laws of the harvest that work in both worlds? Basically, there are three of them. If you can remember these three laws, you will never fail at physical farming. You will never fail in spiritual harvesting, either.

The first fixed law of the harvest is that you reap WHAT you sow. In the natural world, you plant tomatoes to reap tomatoes and you plant cucumbers to reap cucumbers. No farmer ever planted corn in the spring and then harvested wheat in the summer. No farmer ever placed cottonseeds in the ground and then picked squash when the time came to harvest his crops. You reap what you sow. If you plant beans, you pick beans. If you plant radishes, you pull up radishes.

The same is true in the spiritual realm. If you sow hatred, you will be hated. If you sow discord, you will live a discordant life. But if you sow forgiveness, you will reap a lot of forgiveness from God and others. If you sow love, you will be truly loved. If you want to prosper financially, therefore, what "seed" do you need to put in God's spiritual ground? That's right - money! You can't sow kindness and reap a financial harvest. You can't sow mercy and enjoy a crop of financial blessings. The only way you can increase God's financial favor upon your life is by sowing a lot of financial "seeds" in God's kingdom. Then you will reap a financial blessing.

Every seed contains an invisible genetic instruction that determines what that seed will produce. If you could look deep inside the DNA of an apple seed, for example, you would discover a genetic code that is God's created instruction for producing additional apples. Similarly, orange seeds contain a created instruction to produce more oranges. Watermelon seeds, the kind you have to spit out, contain an instruction to produce more watermelons. God determined the harvest when He created the seed, whether the seed was physical or spiritual, and we cannot ignore or change this fixed law of God's creation.

Obviously, like the people Jesus taught when He shared His many parables and metaphors, we understand the natural, physical dimensions of this truth. But we often fail to consider the power of this same truth from a spiritual perspective. When God wanted to cover the earth with fruit trees, He created seeds that were genetically encoded to reproduce those fruit trees. When God wanted to cover the earth with plants and shrubs, He created seeds that contained the necessary "instruction" to reproduce those plants and shrubs (see Genesis 1:11-12). When God wanted to create a family of children in the earth, He sowed his Son, Jesus Christ. He gave His Son an "instruction" to seek and to save that which was lost and to produce a people like Himself in the world by giving His own life and being buried in the earth like a seed.

Jesus had an assignment, an instruction, and a specific purpose, and everything He did was connected to that assignment every day of His earthly life. Through Jesus' death and ensuing resurrection, God produced a family of believers who were destined from the start to be just like Jesus and to reproduce His image in the earth. Just as God sowed a seed for a specific harvest, you and I should sow seeds for a specific harvest. We should sow natural seeds for a specific harvest, and we should sow spiritual seeds for a specific harvest. If we want grace, we should manifest grace. If we want favor *from* men, we should show favor *to* men. And if we want financial blessing, we should demonstrate financial faithfulness and generosity toward the work of God. It's that simple, yet that profound.

There are definite biblical precedents for connecting specific offerings to specific prayer requests, so you can give your offerings an "instruction" and a purpose as you present them to God. In Second Samuel 24, a passage we noted earlier in this chapter, God had struck the nation of Israel with a horrific plague. Approximately 70,000 Israelites had died during three successive days of divine judgment. King David decided to make a sacrifice to the Lord, and he decided to make that sacrifice for the specific purpose of staying God's hand of judgment. So David purchased the threshing floor of Araunah. He purchased Araunah's oxen, too. Then David built an altar and offered his sacrifice. When he did, the plague ceased. David's offering, therefore, had a specific assigned purpose. It had an "instruction," and God honored it.

Another powerful example of this principle can be found in I Kings 17, when Elijah supernaturally provided for a widow at Zarephath and her son. There had been a severe drought in the land, so the woman was running out of food. But God had specifically instructed Elijah to travel to Zarephath, where this woman would supply him with food. When Elijah found the woman, he waxed bold and told her to fix him something to eat, even though he did not know her and even though she was obviously poor. When the woman explained that she had only enough food in her house to prepare one last meal for herself and her son, Elijah told her to give that last meal to him instead. As a result, he said, "The jar of flour will not be used up and the jug of oil will not run dry until the day the LORD gives rain on the land" (I Kings 17:14). Elijah gave this faithful woman a mental picture of what God would do for her if she would sow a seed, if she would give to the Lord out of her apparent lack. If she would give her food to God's prophet, she would reap food in return and she would reap a never-ending supply of it. This woman sowed for a specific harvest. She sowed food for food.

God always gives us specific "seeds" we can sow into His kingdom in order to move His hand on our behalf in a specific area of our lives. In my lifetime, I have sown seeds for healing. I have sown seeds for financial miracles. I have sown seeds for my marriage, for victory in personal struggles, and for much more. The Bible teaches us both implicitly and explicitly that God cannot be bought or bribed. On the other hand, God can be moved. He can be inspired by our faith and touched by our obedience. There is always a seed that we can sow in order to elicit His response in a particular area of our lives, particularly the financial aspects of our lives. If we want financial blessing, we must sow financial seeds. If we want material prosperity, we must sacrifice our present prosperity for the sake of God and His work. The Bible clearly teaches us that we will reap what we sow.

Please don't succumb to the spirit of skepticism that pervades the world today and even affects the hearts and minds of God's people. The world doesn't believe in God or in giving to God's work, and the world certainly doesn't believe that God will bless and prosper those who give. Most people in the world believe that the call to give is a conspiracy by religious charlatans who just want to get their hands on your money. They believe that churches exist only to shake you down and to stockpile wealth. Poor fools! Of course, most of these same people go to their offices every morning and collaborate on how they can get more customers and how they can get more money out of those customers, so they are accustomed to approaching everything from a mindset of greed and manipulation. But, as I have explained, God doesn't need your money and churches don't stockpile cash. God wants your heart and churches send your money out the door as fast as they take it in. The important thing to consider here is yourself, not the motives of church leaders. You need to search your own heart until you clearly understand your own motives. Then you need to repent of any selfishness you might find and learn the grace of godly generosity. You also need to understand that giving is really about your heart, not your wallet. God wants your heart. He knows that your money will follow if He has your heart, and your money will go where it is needed to do the genuine work of God.

So stop listening to the cynics, the doubters, and the mockers. Try tithing for yourself. Plant your financial seeds in the house of God, which is the spiritual "soil" of the kingdom of God (see Psalm 92:13), and see if your efforts don't result in financial favor unlike anything you have ever experienced.

The second fixed law of the harvest is that you reap MORE THAN you sow. A farmer doesn't plant a kernel of corn in the ground so he can reap another kernel later on. He plants a kernel of corn in the ground so he can reap an entire stalk of corn, which will produce thousands of kernels. Similarly, an investor doesn't "plant" his financial seed in an investment portfolio just so he can return in 20 years to retrieve the same amount of money he originally invested. An investor "plants" his financial seed in an investment portfolio so it will grow and produce more money than he put into it.

Everything in God's creation is designed to give the Lord a return on His investment. God created the animals and He commanded them to produce more animals. God created man and He commanded them to produce more human beings. God told the animals to make more animals and He told people to make more people. Likewise, God created the grass to produce more grass and the trees to produce more trees. Jesus even instructed His followers to produce more followers. In fact, Jesus cursed the fig tree that bore no fruit and He punished the servant who refused to invest his master's talent in order to increase his master's wealth (see the parable of the talents in Matthew 25:14-30).

God is displeased when things don't grow and multiply, but He is well pleased when things reproduce. With this in mind, therefore, you can see God's personality at work in the laws of the harvest. A farmer plants one bean in the fertile soil of his farm, and that single bean produces a plant that yields scores of pods filled with hundreds of beans. An investor plants a single dollar in an investment that yields multiple dollars for him, which is then reinvested to earn compound interest that grows those dollars exponentially over the course of the investor's life. You reap *what* you sow, but you also reap *more than* you sow. That's why you sow. That's why you put your "seed" in the ground in the first place. Like God, you want a return on your investment.

Do you give in order to get something back from God? That's an interesting question, and there is no incorrect answer. Some people say, "No! I give to God because I love Him and believe in the work of His kingdom." How noble and how pure! Nevertheless, most of the scriptures in the Bible that deal with giving also carry a strong promise of return on investment, so there is nothing wrong with giving in order to get something back. God said in the book of Malachi, "Bring ye all the tithes into the storehouse… and prove me now herewith… if I will not open you the windows of heaven, and *pour you out a blessing,* that there shall not be room enough to receive it" (Malachi 3:10, KJV, emphasis mine). Jesus said, "Give, and it will be *given to you.* A good measure, pressed down, shaken together and running over, will be *poured into your lap.* For with the measure you use, it will be *measured to you*" (Luke 6:38, emphases mine). So even though it may be a noble thing to give without expecting anything back, God makes it clear that He wants to give back to you when you faithfully give to Him. Now that's favor, and that's reaping more than you sow.

What a great plan! God gives everything to me, then He asks me to give back to Him just the ten percent that belongs to Him anyway so He can know that I acknowledge Him and recognize the source of my wealth. And then, if I will simply give back to Him the ten percent that He already owns, He will open the floodgates of heaven and pour out so many blessings upon my life that I will end up with more than I had when I started giving. To me, that sounds too good to be true. It sounds like I'm taking advantage of God. It sounds like He wants to give me a whole lot more than I will be giving to Him. In fact, if you think about it, I won't really be giving Him anything at all. I'll just be returning to Him a portion of what He gave to me, and then He will give me a lot more back. It's kind of like a money machine, where you can buy a dollar by inserting a dime in the slot. Who wouldn't jump on that offer?

Obviously, I'm being a little facetious here, but the point I am trying to make is that God wants you to prosper. Let me repeat that in case you didn't get it the first time: God wants you to prosper. There is nothing wrong with prosperity. God loves for His people to prosper. But prosperity—the kind of prosperity that comes from above instead of through stressful labor and worry—is directly tied to giving. If you give, God will give back to you. And He will give back to you far more than you ever give to him. That's the law of the harvest.

In God's economy, if you give love, God will give more love back to you. In God's economy, if you show mercy, God will show more mercy to you. If you are patient and kind, God will give you more patience and kindness than you ever show to others. And if you give money, God will give you money in return. In fact, He will give you more money than you ever gave to Him. The law is fixed and is non-negotiable. You reap more than you sow.

The third fixed law of the harvest is that you reap AFTER you sow. I want you to imagine this scene: It's early spring. The faint figure of a lone farmer can be seen walking through the pre-dawn mist as he approaches his plowed field. As he arrives at the edge of the field, he drops a very large and very heavy sack of seeds from his shoulder to the ground. Then kneeling as if he were praying, the farmer looks out across the familiar landscape and begins talking to his field in an audible voice, "Oh field, this has been a very tough year. I want you to know that I have been blessed with this wonderful sack of seeds and there is nothing I would rather do right now than sow these seeds into your fertile soil so I might reap a harvest this summer. But I really need these seeds to eat right now.

"I will make a covenant with you, oh field," the farmer continues. "If you will produce a harvest for me this year—yes, an abundant harvest—I promise you that I will sow seeds into your ground next year during planting season. I vow to do this. I promise, and I am a man of my word. So please help me out here, oh field. Please bless me. Enrich my life and provide me with a bountiful harvest. Then I promise to sow seeds after my circumstances improve."

If you were a local mental health officer and you happened to overhear these words through the early morning fog, you would probably talk to a county judge about locking this farmer up and giving him some much-needed medicine. I would too, because this farmer is obviously living in a delusional world. He is out of touch with reality and could be a danger to himself and others. Yet this is precisely what a lot of Christians do every day when it comes to tithing. They ask God to bless them *first*; then they intend to tithe *afterward*. Unfortunately, the laws of the harvest don't work that way. You have to plant the seeds first; you reap the harvest later on. You reap *after* you sow.

Some people believe they need to increase their income or pay off some of their bills before they can start giving to God. I'm here to tell you that this is backward thinking. God never made one law of tithing for rich people and another law of tithing for poorer people. He did encourage rich people to give alms to the poor, which was a specific responsibility reserved for the more prosperous members of society, but the tithe was universal. Across the board, it was ten percent for everyone, no matter the person's income and no matter the person's temporary plight.

I find it interesting that, although tithing is a biblical principle that appears from Genesis all the way through the epistles of Paul, the act of tithing became a requirement while the Israelites were pilgrims in the wilderness. Just think about that for a moment! God made the practice of tithing a requirement of the law at a time when the Israelites were the poorest they had ever been and the poorest they would ever be. The Jews in the wilderness had no jobs. They had no farms. They manufactured nothing. They produced nothing and they raised nothing. They didn't even have houses to live in, and if God had not supernaturally extended the usefulness of their clothes and their shoes, they would have been naked and barefoot. They even had to rely on God to feed them every morning with manna from heaven because they could not provide simple bread for their families. Yet God commanded them to tithe. He also commanded them to give offerings above and beyond their tithes. In fact, the first offering the Israelites ever gave provided for the construction of the tabernacle, where God met with Moses and where the priests ministered before the Lord. That offering built the house of God, which was elaborate, ornate, and beautiful.

So God doesn't accept the argument that His people need to get their financial affairs in order before they can tithe. He doesn't respond to prayers for blessing when no seeds are being sown in the fertile soil of His house. God's laws are fixed, whether we are talking about the laws of the harvest for the farmer or the laws of the harvest for the giver. You must sow your seeds first; you can expect a return on your investment *afterward*.

Regular giving, like regular planting and plowing, can create a momentum of favor in your life. A farmer cannot plant one year and then decide not to plant the next year. He must be consistent. He must be predictable. The famous *Farmer's Almanac*, which has been around since 1818 and is published every year and not just once in a while when the farmer feels like planting, tells the farmer exactly *when* to plant his seeds and exactly when to harvest his crops. Similarly, the Bible tells us exactly *when* to plant our spiritual seeds ("upon the first day of the week," I Corinthians 16:2, KJV) and *when* to look for our spiritual harvest ("in due season we shall reap, if we faint not," (Galatians 6:9, KJV). The Bible also tells us exactly *how much* to sow ("He which soweth sparingly shall reap also sparingly; and he which soweth bountifully shall reap also bountifully" II Corinthians 9:6, KJV).

When it comes to paying one's tithes and giving one's offerings, the Bible leaves little to chance and little to personal conviction. It tells us what to do and tells us what God will do for us in return. So learn to give, and learn to give properly and with a proper attitude.

Call forth God's financial favor upon your life by connecting yourself with Him through a covenant of giving. Then watch what the Lord does in your life. He owns the cattle on a thousand hills, and since He doesn't personally eat beef, He will gladly share them with you!

THE FORCE OF FAVOR

FAVOR TESTIMONIES

I want to share with you some powerful testimonies from people around the country, people just like you and me, who have heard the principles of favor and have decided to act upon them. In this chapter, your faith will be encouraged and strengthened as you read these testimonies.

"My wife and I had a bill at our doctor's office that we were trying to pay off. He had just built a new office building and needed landscaping done. I own a landscaping company and had thought about trading some landscaping work for the bill we owed. Before I could ask, his office called me and asked if I would be interested in doing the landscaping at the new office for a trade out on our bill. Thank God for favor!"

--Portland, Oregon

"I am a builder who specializes in remodeling. We had two months when business was so slow, and we didn't know what we were going to do. Less than a week after hearing your message on favor and beginning to expect it, we signed jobs on three new houses."

--Little Rock, Arkansas

"I was in one of your meetings and heard you talking about how you can receive favor on your job. I decided to try it, and it worked. Less than five days after I sowed a financial seed and wrote 'job promotion' on the check, my boss called me in and told me he wanted to give me a promotion. Then he told me I was not only going to get a promotion, but I was going to get a raise, as well. My salary just went from $25,000 to $43,000 a year. Thank God for His favor!"

--Tampa, Florida

"When you spoke at my church, I sowed a seed for favor. The next morning the stock market had a significant drop, and people lost thousands of dollars. My stock went up thousands. That is the favor of God."

--San Francisco, California

"I sowed a seed for favor on my business. We were just beginning and needed some customers. I had a meeting with a prospective customer the day after I sowed my seed. I confessed favor, and I walked out with the job."

--Hickory, North Carolina

"After being set free from drugs and getting involved with my church, I decided that I wanted to be an usher. I didn't have the money to go and buy several suits, so I thought I would just buy one and that would be a start. My wife and I picked one out and took it to have alterations done. When we went back to pick it up, the man at the alterations place asked me if I would like two more suits. Someone had dropped them off over 90 days earlier and had never picked them up. They were both my exact size."

--Irving, Texas

"I had been trying to find a new job and had been for several interviews. You spoke on declaring favor when you go for a job interview. I had an interview the next morning, and I decided to try it. It worked! I not only got the job, but more pay than I was asking for. Praise the Lord for His favor."

--Dallas, Texas

"I had been on my job as a part-time employee for just a couple of months. There were around 20 people waiting to go full-time, and most of those people were ahead of me. I became a monthly 'favor partner' with your ministry and the next week, my boss called me in and asked me if I would like to go full-time. He said he would move me to the top of the list if I wanted him to. I said, 'of course I would.' It was only two weeks later that I was promoted to supervisor. The other supervisor had been with the company four years before becoming a supervisor, and I was made one in four months. Favor will accelerate your destiny. Thank you for teaching this powerful message."

--St. Petersburg, Florida

"I had never thought about the favor of God bringing healing to my body until you shared about Sarah in the Bible. I took hold of that and asked God to show me favor by healing my body. I had suffered with tremendous pain and arthritis in my legs and hips. I asked God to show me favor and take this pain from me and heal me, and He did. Today I am totally healed, and there is no more pain."

--Chicago, Illinois

"I had a school loan for $23,000 that I was trying to pay off. I had just made my first payment on this loan, but my desire was to pay it off quickly. I wanted God to show me favor in this situation. I planted a financial seed when you were at our church and God moved quicker than I ever imagined. Within five days, I received a letter from the school loan company which stated that they had received my payment, and, pending the processing of it, they were marking my bill 'paid in full.' I couldn't believe it—$23,000 of debt canceled."

--Orlando, Florida

"I had heard you preach at our church before, but never really believed all the stuff about sowing and reaping. The last time you were there, something told me to try it and see what would happen. I gave an offering that night and within ten days, $5000 was deposited directly into my account. I thought it must have been a mistake, but later found out it was an inheritance from a relative who had died several years earlier. I had forgotten they were still dealing with the estate. It works, and thank you for sharing. From this day forward, I will never doubt God's favor."

--Kokomo, Indiana

"The first time that I heard you speak about the favor of God, I sowed a financial seed into your ministry for favor in a relationship. I needed God to show me favor and somehow bring restoration. God began to move, and, in just a few short weeks, that relationship was restored and is growing stronger every day. Praise God! I believe in sowing seed, especially in a ministry that is producing the kind of results you are."

--Hudson, Florida

"My husband and I had been trying to have a child for years. We had been to clinics and tried everything, then you came to our church and shared your message on favor. We had not tried that. We had prayed, but we had never asked God for favor. Well, that night you laid hands on us and prayed for God to show us favor, and He did. I am now four months pregnant, and things are great. Thank you so much for being obedient to the Holy Spirit and sharing the message of favor."

--Denver, Colorado

"I had a debt of $65,000 from a business deal that I had done. I didn't feel that I owed this money, that it was not right. I spoke with the bank, and they told me they would research it. I was in one of your 'Favor Friday' meetings and planted a $1,000 seed for favor in this situation. Within ten days, I received a call from the vice president of the bank. He said there had been a mistake. I did not owe the bank $65,000, but they actually owed me $27,600. They cut the check that day and overnighted it."

--Orlando, Florida

"My business was doing well, and I was satisfied with my financial income. Then you came into my life and encouraged me to reach for increase and favor. Within a few weeks of sowing into your ministry, I got a new client who was worth one million dollars a year. That one client doubled the income of my entire company. I just met with that client again last week, and they raised their business with me from one million to three million dollars a year."

--Irving, Texa

"I had a debt of $1500 that I owed a man in my church. When you were ministering at our church, I decided to sow the $111 seed that you were talking about, even though I had several bills that I owed. I knew that $111 would not pay off my bills, so I sowed it. I did that in the service that morning. After service that night, the man I owed walked up to me and said that God told him to forgive my debt."

--Wheaton, Illinois

s*"I had just moved to the States from Costa Rica with my family when you came to our church. I had just found a job and a place to live. We needed furniture, but could not afford it at the time. I went to work the day after you laid hands on us, and my boss told me to take the truck and pick up some things. He told me where to go, and I went to the place. They filled my truck with new furniture, and I went back. My boss told me the furniture was for my family and me. Praise the Lord."*

--Hickory, North Carolina

"When you were at our church, I sowed a $111 seed into your ministry. My family was getting ready to make a move out of state and needed all the money we had. But we obeyed God and sowed. As soon as church was over, someone handed me a $111 check and said, 'God told me to give this to you.' After church, we went out to eat with a family. By the end of our lunch, the man had handed me ten $100 bills. That's $1,000! So in less than three hours after sowing my $111 seed, God blessed me with $1,111."

--Montgomery, Alabama

THE FORCE OF FAVOR

MEMORY SCRIPTURES

In this section, you will find 52 scriptural references on favor, one for each week of the year. I recommend that you read each scripture every day for seven consecutive days. I also recommend that you memorize as many of these passages as possible in order to strengthen your command of God's Word and equip yourself to see God's hand of favor on your life. These scripture references are listed in order, from Genesis through the writings of Paul, and are taken from the New International Version of the Bible.

WEEK 1

But Abel brought fat portions from some of the firstborn of his flock. The LORD looked with favor on Abel and his offering.

Genesis 4:4

WEEK 2

So the LORD said, "I will wipe mankind, whom I have created, from the face of the earth--men and animals, and creatures that move along the ground, and birds of the air--for I am grieved that I have made them." But Noah found favor in the eyes of the LORD.

Genesis 6:7–8

WEEK 3

He said, "If I have found favor in your eyes, my lord, do not pass your servant by. Let a little water be brought, and then you may all wash your feet and rest under this tree. Let me get you something to eat, so you can be refreshed and then go on your way-- now that you have come to your servant."

"Very well," they answered, "do as you say."

Genesis 18:3–5

WEEK 4

The LORD was with Joseph and he prospered, and he lived in the house of his Egyptian master. When his master saw that the LORD was with him and that the LORD gave him success in everything he did, Joseph found favor in his eyes and became his attendant. Potiphar put him in charge of his household, and he entrusted to his care everything he owned. From the time he put him in charge of his household and of all that he owned, the LORD blessed the household of the Egyptian because of Joseph. The blessing of the LORD was on everything Potiphar had, both in the house and in the field. So he left in Joseph's care everything he had; with Joseph in charge, he did not concern himself with anything except the food he ate.

Genesis 39:2-6

WEEK 5

Joseph's master took him and put him in prison, the place where the king's prisoners were confined. But while Joseph was there in the prison, the LORD was with him; he showed him kindness and granted him favor in the eyes of the prison warden. So the warden put Joseph in charge of all those held in the prison, and he was made responsible for all that was done there. The warden paid no attention to anything under Joseph's care, because the LORD was with Joseph and gave him success in whatever he did.

Genesis 39:20-23

WEEK 6

And I will make the Egyptians favorably disposed toward this people, so that when you leave you will not go empty-handed.

Exodus 3:21

WEEK 7

The LORD made the Egyptians favorably disposed toward the people, and Moses himself was highly regarded in Egypt by Pharaoh's officials and by the people.

Exodus 11:3

WEEK 8

The LORD had made the Egyptians favorably disposed toward the people, and they gave them what they asked for; so they plundered the Egyptians.

Exodus 12:36

WEEK 9

Moses said to the LORD, "You have been telling me, 'Lead these people,' but you have not let me know whom you will send with me. You have said, 'I know you by name and you have found favor with me.' If you are pleased with me, teach me your ways so I may know you and continue to find favor with you. Remember that this nation is your people."

Exodus 33:12-13

WEEK 10

"O Lord, if I have found favor in your eyes," he said, "then let the Lord go with us. Although this is a stiff-necked people, forgive our wickedness and our sin, and take us as your inheritance." Then the LORD said: "I am making a covenant with you. Before all your people I will do wonders never before done in any nation in all the world. The people you live among will see how awesome is the work that I, the LORD, will do for you."

Exodus 34:9-10

WEEK 11

I will look on you with favor and make you fruitful and increase your numbers, and I will keep my covenant with you.

Leviticus 26:9

WEEK 12

The LORD bless you and keep you; the LORD make his face shine upon you and be gracious to you; the LORD turn his face toward you and give you peace.

Numbers 6:24-26

WEEK 13

Gideon replied, "If now I have found favor in your eyes, give me a sign that it is really you talking to me. Please do not go away until I come back and bring my offering and set it before you." And the LORD said, "I will wait until you return."

Judges 6:17–18

WEEK 14

At this, she bowed down with her face to the ground. She exclaimed, "Why have I found such favor in your eyes that you notice me–a foreigner?... May I continue to find favor in your eyes, my lord," she said. "You have given me comfort and have spoken kindly to your servant–though I do not have the standing of one of your servant girls."

Ruth 2:10, 13

WEEK 15

And the boy Samuel continued to grow in stature and in favor with the LORD and with men.

I Samuel 2:26

WEEK 16

May the LORD now show you kindness and faithfulness, and I too will show you the same favor because you have done this.

II Samuel 2:6

WEEK 17

Then Jehoahaz sought the LORD's favor, and the LORD listened to him, for he saw how severely the king of Aram was oppressing Israel.

II Kings 13:4

WEEK 18

In his distress he sought the favor of the LORD his God and humbled himself greatly before the God of his fathers.

II Chronicles 33:12

WEEK 19

When the turn came for Esther (the girl Mordecai had adopted, the daughter of his uncle Abihail) to go to the king, she asked for nothing other than what Hegai, the king's eunuch who was in charge of the harem, suggested. And Esther won the favor of everyone who saw her.

Esther 2:15–16

WEEK 20

Then Queen Esther answered, "If I have found favor with you, O king, and if it pleases your majesty, grant me my life-this is my petition. And spare my people-this is my request."

Esther 7:3

WEEK 21

He prays to God and finds favor with him, he sees God's face and shouts for joy; he is restored by God to his righteous state.

Job 33:26

WEEK 22

Many are asking, "Who can show us any good?" Let the light of your face shine upon us, O LORD.

Psalm 4:6

WEEK 23

For surely, O LORD, you bless the righteous; you surround them with your favor as with a shield.

Psalm 5:12

WEEK 24

For his anger lasts only a moment, but his favor lasts a lifetime; weeping may remain for a night, but rejoicing comes in the morning.

Psalm 30:5

WEEK 25

Let your face shine on your servant; save me in your unfailing love.

Psalm 31:16

WEEK 26

The king is enthralled by your beauty; honor him, for he is your lord. The Daughter of Tyre will come with a gift, men of wealth will seek your favor.

Psalm 45:11–12

WEEK 27

May God be gracious to us and bless us and make his face shine upon us.

Psalm 67:1

WEEK 28

Restore us, O God; make your face shine upon us, that we may be saved.

Psalm 80:3

WEEK 29

You showed favor to your land, O LORD; you restored the fortunes of Jacob.

Psalm 85:1

WEEK 30

For you are their glory and strength,
and by your favor you exalt our horn.

Psalm 89:17

WEEK 31

May the favor of the Lord our God rest upon us; establish the work of our hands for us--yes, establish the work of our hands.

Psalm 90:17

WEEK 32

You will arise and have compassion on Zion, for it is time to show favor to her; the appointed time has come.

Psalm 102:13

WEEK 33

Make your face shine upon your servant and teach me your decrees.

Psalm 119:135

WEEK 34

Let love and faithfulness never leave you; bind them around your neck, write them on the tablet of your heart. Then you will win favor and a good name in the sight of God and man.

Proverbs 3:3–4

WEEK 35

Now then, my sons, listen to me; blessed are those who keep my ways. Listen to my instruction and be wise; do not ignore it. Blessed is the man who listens to me, watching daily at my doors, waiting at my doorway. For whoever finds me finds life and receives favor from the LORD.

Proverbs 8:32–35

WEEK 36

A good man obtains favor from the LORD, but the LORD condemns a crafty man.

Proverbs 12:2

WEEK 37

Good understanding wins favor, but the way of the unfaithful is hard.

Proverbs 13:15

WEEK 38

He who finds a wife finds what is good and receives favor from the LORD.

Proverbs 18:22

WEEK 39

Many curry favor with a ruler, and everyone is the friend of a man who gives gifts.

Proverbs 19:6

WEEK 40

Yet the LORD longs to be gracious to you; he rises to show you compassion. For the LORD is a God of justice. Blessed are all who wait for him!

Isaiah 30:18

WEEK 41

Foreigners will rebuild your walls, and their kings will serve you. Though in anger I struck you, in favor I will show you compassion. Your gates will always stand open, they will never be shut, day or night, so that men may bring you the wealth of the nations--their kings led in triumphal procession.

Isaiah 60:10-11

WEEK 42

The Spirit of the Sovereign LORD is on me, because the LORD has anointed me to preach good news to the poor. He has sent me to bind up the brokenhearted, to proclaim freedom for the captives and release from darkness for the prisoners, to proclaim the year of the LORD's favor.

Isaiah 61:1-2

WEEK 43

But Daniel resolved not to defile himself with the royal food and wine, and he asked the chief official for permission not to defile himself this way. Now God had caused the official to show favor and sympathy to Daniel.

Daniel 1:8-9

WEEK 44

The angel went to her and said, "Greetings, you who are highly favored! The Lord is with you." Mary was greatly troubled at his words and wondered what kind of greeting this might be. But the angel said to her, "Do not be afraid, Mary, you have found favor with God."

Luke 1:28-30

WEEK 45

Glory to God in the highest, and on earth peace to men on whom his favor rests.

Luke 2:14

WEEK 46

And Jesus grew in wisdom and stature, and in favor with God and men.

Luke 2:52

WEEK 47

The Spirit of the Lord is on me, because he has anointed me to preach good news to the poor. He has sent me to proclaim freedom for the prisoners and recovery of sight for the blind, to release the oppressed, to proclaim the year of the Lord's favor.

Luke 4:18-19

WEEK 48

Every day they continued to meet together in the temple courts. They broke bread in their homes and ate together with glad and sincere hearts, praising God and enjoying the favor of all the people. And the Lord added to their number daily those who were being saved.

Acts 2:46-47

WEEK 49

Because the patriarchs were jealous of Joseph, they sold him as a slave into Egypt. But God was with him and rescued him from all his troubles. He gave Joseph wisdom and enabled him to gain the goodwill of Pharaoh king of Egypt; so he made him ruler over Egypt and all his palace.

Acts 7:9-10

WEEK 50

Having received the tabernacle, our fathers under Joshua brought it with them when they took the land from the nations God drove out before them. It remained in the land until the time of David, who enjoyed God's favor and asked that he might provide a dwelling place for the God of Jacob.

Acts 7:45-46

WEEK 51

For he says, "In the time of my favor I heard you, and in the day of salvation I helped you." I tell you, now is the time of God's favor, now is the day of salvation.

II Corinthians 6:2

WEEK 52

The Spirit of the Sovereign LORD is on me, because the LORD has anointed me to preach good news to the poor. He has sent me to bind up the brokenhearted, to proclaim freedom for the captives and release from darkness for the prisoners, to proclaim the year of the LORD's favor.

Isaiah 61:1-2

THE FORCE OF FAVOR

FAVOR FACTS

Favor is the greatest harvest you could ever receive from God.

Favor will determine the level of your income.

Favor will show up in your life when you associate with the right people.

Favor will cause you to regain in one day what the enemy has stolen for years.

Favor is a spendable commodity. God gives you favor so you can help advance the kingdom.

Favor must be a seed before it becomes a harvest.

Favor will become a shield of protection around your life.

Favor comes when you concentrate on the success of others.

Favor that is not celebrated will become favor lost.

Favor will increase when you put others ahead of yourself.

You can lose favor just as quickly as you gained it.

Favor will cause your medical reports to change.

A day of favor will change your life forever.

Favor will cause you to rise to the top in whatever you do.

Favor will accelerate your destiny.

When you declare God's favor with your mouth,
that favor will increase.

Favor is a reward for obedience.

Spending time in prayer with God will increase your favor.

The closer you are to someone, the more willing they will be to show
you favor.

One day of favor is worth a thousand days of labor.

Favor will increase the moment you solve a problem for someone.

Excellence will increase your favor with God and man.

When you plant a seed of favor, you can expect a harvest of favor.

Tithing is a door to financial favor.

Favor will always bring you to the top.

Favor is not merely an event, it is a lifestyle.

Favor can be lost as quickly as it was received.

This year and every year is the year of the Lord's favor.

Favor will lead you where God wants to take you.

Favor will leave your life when you associate with the wrong people.

Favor could be the hidden ingredient to restoration in relationships.

PRAYER OF SALVATION

God loves you—no matter who you are, no matter what your past. God loves you so much that He gave His one and only begotten Son for you. The Bible tells us that "...whoever believes in him shall not perish but have eternal life" (John 3:16 NIV). Jesus laid down His life and rose again so that we could spend eternity with Him in heaven and experience His absolute best on earth. If you would like to receive Jesus into your life, say the following prayer out loud and mean it from your heart.

Heavenly Father, I come to You admitting that I am a sinner. Right now, I choose to turn away from sin, and I ask You to cleanse me of all unrighteousness. I believe that Your Son, Jesus, died on the cross to take away my sins. I also believe that He rose again from the dead so that I might be forgiven of my sins and be made righteous through faith in Him. I call upon the name of Jesus Christ to be the Savior and Lord of my life. Jesus, I choose to follow You and ask that You fill me with the power of the Holy Spirit. I declare that right now I am a child of God. I am free from sin and full of the righteousness of God. I am saved in Jesus' name. Amen.

If you prayed this prayer to receive Jesus Christ as your Savior for the first time, please contact us on the Web at www.harrison-house.com to receive a free book.

ABOUT THE AUTHOR

Dr. Dave Martin is known by many around the world as America's #1 Christian Success Coach. He has embraced his assignment to teach others how to walk in the fullness of God's plan by pursuing, possessing and teaching the scriptural keys to biblical success.

His Ultimate Life Seminars attract thousands of people each year from across the country and around the world. He regularly appears on INSP, TBN, Daystar, and many other television programs.

Dr. Dave is the author of several bestselling books including *The Force of Favor* which teaches people to recognize, accept, and walk in the favor of God, and *Name Your It*, a teaching on the power of a seed. Most recently he released *Creating the Ultimate Life*, a 20-CD series and workbook, which teaches you to "Stop making a LIVING and start making a LIFE!"

Dr. Dave is a husband, father, author, inspirational speaker, successful businessman, and national television host. He speaks regularly in churches, colleges and business organizations. Dr. Dave's powerful life improvement messages have been embraced by God's people, political figures, kings and presidents, professional athletes, actors, and Fortune 500 companies.

His wife, Christine, is a powerful teacher speaking regularly in conferences and women's meetings.

Their international headquarters is located in beautiful Orlando, Florida.

Follow me.

Keep in touch with live events, timely coaching and ministry in your area!

Twitter   Facebook   Vimeo

@drdavemartin   /davemartininternational   /drdavemartin

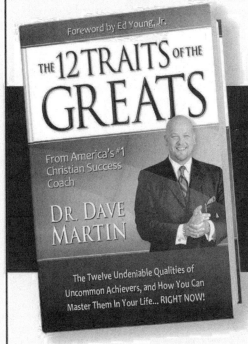

The Harrison House Vision

Proclaiming the truth and the power

Of the Gospel of Jesus Christ

With excellence;

Challenging Christians to

Live victoriously,

Grow spiritually,

Know God intimately.